# Declutter Your Life

## 2 in 1

*The Keys to Decluttering Your Life and Reduce Stress: Includes Declutter Your Home and Declutter Your Mind*

Mary Connor

# Copyright 2018 © Mary Connor

All rights reserved.

No part of this guide may be reproduced in any form without permission in writing from the publisher except in the case of review.

## Legal & Disclaimer

The following document is reproduced below with the goal of providing information that is as accurate and reliable as possible.

This declaration is deemed fair and valid by both the American Bar Association and the Committee of Publishers Association and is legally binding throughout the United States.

Furthermore, the transmission, duplication or reproduction of any of the following work including specific information will be considered an illegal act irrespective of if it is done electronically or in print. This extends to creating a secondary or tertiary copy of the work or a recorded copy and is only allowed with an express written consent from the Publisher. All additional right reserved.

The information in the following pages is broadly considered to be a truthful and accurate account of facts, and as such any inattention, use or misuse of the information in question by the reader will render any resulting actions solely under their purview. There are no scenarios in which the publisher or the original author of this work can be in any fashion deemed liable for any hardship or damages that may befall them after undertaking information described herein.

Additionally, the information in the following pages is intended only for informational purposes and should thus be thought of as universal. As befitting its nature, it is presented without assurance regarding its prolonged validity or interim quality. Trademarks that are mentioned are done without written consent and can in no way be considered an endorsement from the trademark holder.

# Table of Contents

# Book 1: Declutter Your Home

Introduction ..................................................11

Chapter 1: What is Minimalism? ............................15

Chapter 2: What is a Decluttering Mindset? ...........26

Chapter 3: Top 10 Reasons Why You Haven't Started Decluttering Already ...................................34

Chapter 4: Top 10 Benefits of Turning Your Decluttering Into a Habit.........................................42

Chapter 5: How to Organize Your Time to Make Decluttering Easier ................................................53

    How to Create a Weekly Organizing Routine......54

    Management Tips When Decluttering Your Home................................................................59

Chapter 6: How to Set Your Priorities When Housekeeping and How to Create a Plan ................64

Chapter 7: The Steps You Need to Declutter the Kitchen..................................................................71

    Simple Steps to Help You Declutter the Kitchen Quickly..................................................72

    Some Easy Tips to Help You Organize the Kitchen ................................................................77

    Maintaining the Kitchen Clean...........................83

Chapter 8: Decluttering the Common Living Space ............................................. 85
   How to Declutter the Living Room ...................... 86
   The Four Looks Decluttering Method ................. 89
   Tips to Help You Get Even More Out of Your Living Room ........................................................ 91

Chapter 9: The Dreaded Bathrooms and How to Make Them More Manageable ............................... 96
   The ABC's of bathroom storage .......................... 97
   Some Tips to Make Decluttering Your Bathroom Easier ................................................ 101

Chapter 10: Cleaning Up the Bedrooms ................. 107
   Getting Rid of the Extra Things that are in your Room .......................................................... 108
   Keeping Up with the Maintenance of the Cleaning ............................................................ 114

Chapter 11: Watch Out for Those Lego! – How to Declutter Your Kids' Rooms ............................... 117

Chapter 12: Working on the Office for a More Effective You ........................................................ 124
   Identify How You Plan to Use the Office and What is the Most Important ............................. 124
   Remove Anything that is a Household or Personal Item ...................................................... 127
   Declutter the Workstation ................................. 128

Make a Checklist for Decluttering ................... 130

Chapter 13: Cleaning Out the Garage and the Basement ............................................................... 134

    Decluttering the Garage .................................. 135

    Decluttering the Basement ............................. 139

Chapter 14: How to Make That Closet Look Organized ............................................................ 145

Chapter 15: Daily Tips to Make Decluttering Your Life Easier ..................................................... 154

Chapter 16: Different Techniques You Can Use to Make Decluttering a Breeze ........................... 164

    KonMarie Method ............................................ 164

    The Minimalist Game ....................................... 166

    The Four Box Method ...................................... 168

    One Method ...................................................... 170

    Packing Party .................................................... 171

    The Closet Hanger Method ............................. 173

Conclusion ................................................................ 176

# Book 2: Declutter Your Mind

Introduction ............................................................. 180
Chapter 1: Why People Live With Cluttered
Minds ..................................................................... 186
Chapter 2: What Happens When We Are
Overwhelmed With So Much Social Media ........... 193
   How Mental Clutter Can Create Chaos in
   Your Life ............................................................. 195
   The Effect of Stress on Your Body ..................... 200
Chapter 3: Tips to Limit Your Overwhelm and
Be More Productive. ............................................... 207
   Limiting Your Information Overload ................ 207
   Decluttering your social media usage ............... 218
   Clearing Out Your Email Inbox ......................... 219
   Uninstalling Software You Do Not Need ........... 221
   Clearing the Junk on Your Phone ...................... 223
Chapter 4: How Decluttering Can Improve Your
Relationships ......................................................... 225
   How Decluttering Can Improve Your Anxiety .. 226
   Improving Your Attitude Towards Others In
   Your Life ............................................................. 227
   Decluttering Your Relationships ....................... 228
   How to Identify a Bad Influence and Then
   Subsequently Illuminate Them ......................... 231

Allowing Yourself To Cut Ties With Negative Influences............................................................239

Chapter 5: Breaking the Habit of Multitasking And Alternatives for Stress Reduction ..................242

    Breaking the Habit of Multitasking....................245

    Exercise is another way to eliminate stress........255

Chapter 6: Relieve Stress By Eating Healthy, Adding Healthy Habits And Utilizing Meditation..............................................................272

    Breathing Exercises That Work..........................273

    Making healthier food choices can help eliminate stress and overwhelm........................278

Chapter 7: Decluttering Your Thoughts By Keeping A Journal................................................297

Chapter 8: Reframing Negative Thought Patterns ..............................................................319

    Consider what your core values are and how you can prioritize them. ......................................321

    3 Ways to Change These Core Beliefs.................329

    Working Towards Goals That Will Improve Your Life...............................................................332

    Strategies to Practice Positive Thinking.............333

Chapter 9: Creating Healthier Routines and Daily Habits for Anxiety and Stress Relief ............335

    Scheduling a New Daily Routine .......................335

Be more active and stress less, gain more sleep, and live with less clutter ........................... 345
Supplements provide a great way to maximize your health and create a protective barrier for stress. ................................................ 351
Conclusion .............................................................. 353
Workbook ............................................................... 359
About the Author .................................................... 380

# Book 1:
# Declutter Your Home

The Ridiculously Thorough Guide to Decluttering Your Home, Organizing Your Work Space and Living the Minimalist Lifestyle without Going Overboard

# Introduction

The world that we live in now is full of things, of material possessions. We are bombarded with advertisements all of the time, ones telling us that we need to have this item or that item. It is a way for big companies to make a lot of money, and they promise us it will help make us happy, help us make friends, and help us have a better life.

In reality, none of this is true. Most of us spend more and more money on material possessions and find out that it leaves us feeling empty inside. It takes up a lot of our time as we work more to purchase more items, we clean up more to get those items out of our way, and we assign too much power and emotions to those items because they are all we are connected to. This can lead to a real problem that many people don't even know that they are dealing with.

When you decide that it is time to declutter, you will start making some drastic changes to your life. Minimalism is an idea that hasn't caught on yet too much of the modern world, but the idea that you can actually be happy, that you can slow down in life, and really enjoy things and feel less stress, is very comforting and positive to a lot of people. And the process of decluttering different parts of your life can really help to make this a reality.

This guidebook is going to talk a bit more about decluttering and all the benefits that come with it. We start out with an explanation of minimalism, and how it can be a great way to help you live your life to the fullest. Minimalism is different for everyone, and despite popular belief, it doesn't mean that you need to get rid of everything that you own. Minimalism can mean different things to each person, as long as you make intentional decisions about things you purchase and only go for the ones that actually make you happy.

After talking about minimalism, we will spend some time looking into decluttering. We will look at some of the benefits of doing this in your home, some of the reasons that people have yet to start with decluttering, and the importance of managing your time and setting up a routine to keep the decluttering process going.

This all leads up to some practical steps that you can take to clean up every room in your home. We will take a look at how to clean the kitchen, the bathrooms, the bedrooms, the living rooms, the office, your garage and basement, and even those messy closets. While you should take this process slowly to help prevent yourself from becoming overwhelmed, by the time you are done with this guidebook, you are going to see a vast improvement in the cleanliness of your home, in the amount of clutter that is present, and the amount of freed and stress that you feel in your life.

We will then end with some of the different decluttering methods that you can use, including some that have become very popular, and can help you get the most out of your decluttering session.

Many people avoid decluttering their lives because they are worried about how long it will take, they add too much value to the items they own, or they just don't want to handle it at all. With the help of this guidebook, you will be able to declutter your home and finally find the peace and stress relief that you have been looking for.

# Chapter 1: What is Minimalism?

Before we get started with the idea of decluttering, it is important to understand minimalism and how it can come into play. It is actually quite simple. It is the idea that you live with as little as possible. Instead of getting involved in a culture that is all about purchasing more things, and trying to keep up with your neighbors, and purchase more materials goods. While many people hear the word minimalism and assume it means they can't have a home, or a car, and never travel or do anything, and only one a handful of items, this is kind of to the extreme. Minimalism doesn't mean you have to live in a hole and have nothing. It just means that you learn what you really need to survive, without all the extra stuff that just takes up space.

Minimalism is a tool that is going to assist you in finding freedom that you could never imagine. It can provide you with some freedom from fear, worry, from being overwhelmed, and even from guilt and depression. Even better, it can help you gain some freedom from the trappings of the consumer culture, that most people have built their lives around.

This doesn't mean that there is something really bad about owning material possessions. If you actually use those items and find real enjoyment from them, then they are great. But the problem comes when we give too much meaning to the things that we own, giving so much attention to these things than our personal growth, our passions, our relationships, and our health. It becomes a problem when we have things just to have them there, without having them actually do anything for you.

It is fine to own a home, raise a family, and have material possessions when you are a minimalist. This is not about getting rid of everything. But it is a method that helps you to make these decisions, decisions about what you purchase and own, in a more deliberate and conscious manner.

There are lots of people who are successful with being a minimalist who are able to lead an appreciably different life. There are different types of minimalists who do well. Some like to keep themselves down to just a few possessions and nothing else, mainly to make life simpler and to keep them away from materialistic thoughts. But there are plenty of these minimalists who have cars, homes, families, careers, and more, they simply just learn how to make smart and deliberate decisions about material objects before they make a purchase.

The next question that you may have is how people can be so different and still be considered minimalists. This can bring us back to the first question that we asked — "What is minimalism?" This can be complicated to describe, but to keep it simple, minimalism is a tool that can help you get rid of the excesses in life in favor of focusing on what is important so you can find freedom, fulfillment, and happiness.

There are a lot of things that minimalism is able to help you out with many different things including:

- Helps you grow as an individual
- Focus more on your health
- Create more and consume less
- Experience some real freedom

- Discover the mission that you should really have in life
- Pursue your passions
- Live in the moment rather than focusing on the future or the past so much
- Reclaim some of our time since you don't have to worry about cleaning nonstop
- Eliminate some of the discontents on our lives
- Discover your purpose in life
- Rid your life of all the extra stuff that is just in the way
- Be able to contribute to the world beyond ourselves

When you learn how to incorporate minimalism into your life, even just a little bit, it provides you with a way to find lasting happiness, and this is what everyone is really looking for. We all want to be happy. But while other people focus on finding happiness through the different things that they own, a minimalist is going to search for happiness through their life and the memories they make. This means that you get the benefit of choosing what is necessary, and what is superfluous in your own life.

Minimalism has the possibility to be different for every person. Some people will use it as a way to help them keep their life in order and actually enjoy things. But for some people, a good life includes lots of books so they will make sure they have a large library around them. Some people like to take trips with their families and will use their money towards that. Just because you have a few things in your life and you don't live like a monk to be considered a minimalist in your life.

A few things to consider when it comes to figuring out what minimalism is and how you can bring it into your life include:

- **It is about intentionality**: Minimalism is marked with intentionality, purpose, and clarity. At the core, this idea is all about the intentional promotion of the things that we already value the most, and the removal of everything that will take our attention away from it. This type of life means that you need to be intentional with what you do so that you see marked improvements in all parts of your life.

- **It provides you with some freedom from the passion that you have to possess items**: Our modern culture has taught us that the only way that you can have a good life is when you accumulate more things. The more you own, the happier you will be. But this is a very false idea. This can actually trap us, making us value items too much, making us follow these items and what is the latest trend, and dealing with all the debt that comes with this. Minimalism is going to bring you some freedom from the all-consuming passion that most people have to possess more items. This lifestyle is going to let us step off the treadmill of consumerism, and helps you to seek more happiness in other places. You can then start to value your self-care, the experiences you have, and your relationships.

- **It offers you some freedom from many modern manias**: Our modern world moves at a feverish pace. We always rush around and feel stressed, we work long hours to pay the bills, and still fall more into debt. We are always running around and being busy, but we can't form good relationships, or ever relax and enjoy the things that we have. Minimalism is great because it helps us to slow down our lives and reduce some of the stress that we feel. We get the freedom to disengage, it allows us to get rid of anything that is frivolous, and can make it easier to just find endeavors that add some value to our lives.

- **It offers freedom from duplicity**: Although no one really chooses it, most people live in duplicity. They live one life around their neighbors, one around their co-workers, and one around their family. This is due to the lifestyle that they choose. But with minimalism, you are able to choose a life that is simple, one that is consistent and united. You can have the same kind of lifestyle no matter who you are around, and this can make things so much easier.

- **It is counter-cultural**: Right now, we are in a world that idolizes celebrities. Their lives are held up as the standard that everyone should live by. Those who have a minimalist life are not shown by the media, because they don't fit into the current consumerist culture that politicians and corporations try to promote. While most people are going for fame, success, and more possessions, minimalism is going to ask you to slow down, consume more, but still enjoy your life more. And after following this kind of lifestyle for just a short amount of time, it is easy to see that we have made the right decision and that this method is way better compared to the way we did before.

- **Minimalism is more internal**: Minimalism is more a matter of the heart than anything else. After all that clutter externally has been removed, minimalism has the space to address the way that we live our lives and enjoy our relationships. And in some cases, those outside of our family may not even recognize that we have taken on this kind of lifestyle. But if you learn how to declutter, and only live with the things that you need and that make you truly happy, you are going to find your life can be quite different than before.

- **It is achievable**: Despite what our current culture may tell us, minimalism is achievable. We don't need to have the latest and greatest gadget. We don't need to fill our homes with a ton of things to make us happy. What we need is our family, or friends, and a few other things to help us have the happy life that we need. Minimalism can help you to reach that goal and reach the ultimate happiness that you want.

Minimalism is an idea that is a bit different from what our modern society tells us what is normal. While others are following the latest trend and trying to get as many possessions as possible, you could be living your best and happiest life simply by following the idea of minimalism.

# Chapter 2: What is a Decluttering Mindset?

Before you get started on your method of decluttering, it is important to realize that this takes a certain type of mindset. If you are too attached to your items, or you start out feeling that you will only get rid of a few things, or that this is going to be too difficult to accomplish, then things are not going to go the way that you plan. Having a certain mindset ahead of time can make a big difference in how much you can accomplish.

Some of the things that you should consider when you get started with your own decluttering and help you with a decluttering mindset include:

- **Make decisions quickly**: The longer you think about something, the more likely it is that you will keep that item in your home, even if you never use it. The first reaction that you have to an item should be the one that you go with. Give yourself 30 seconds or less on each item. Make the decision and don't look back.

- **Have a clear list of criteria that help you to make decisions**: Before you get started with decluttering, take some time to write out a list of the criteria you will follow, when you get rid of, or keep things. Then, as you go through each room, keep this list on hand. If the item doesn't meet your criteria, it is time to get rid of it.

- **Pick a day when you are ready**: If you have a stressful week at work, if you are feeling sick, or if you really don't feel doing any decluttering, it is fine to hold off starting or take a break along the way. Sometimes you may need to give yourself some time before you continue on in the process. Just take that break and get back to it as soon as possible. Enter into the process of decluttering with a can-do attitude and you will be able to get the work done.

- **Have limits on how much of the sentimental stuff can stick around**: Sentimental stuff is great, and it is fine to keep a few of them around. This is especially good if you actually use them in some manner in your home. For example, if you have a wall clock that your grandfather gave you and you still use it, then it is fine to keep it around. But there is a limit to how much of this sentimental stuff should stick around. Pick a number of how many you are comfortable with and then get rid of everything else.

- **Have a wait and see box**: There are going to be some items that you are not sure what you want to do with right that moment. You should try to make firm decisions with your stuff, deciding whether to keep or get rid of them right away. But there may be a few things that you are uncertain about. Instead of putting it back into your closet or back in the room, put it in your wait and see box. Then, if you don't use it within a few months, it is time to get rid of that item because you don't really need it.

- **Don't allow obligation or guilt with presents**: One issue that can come up when you get started with decluttering is guilt or a sense of obligation when someone gives you a gift. You don't want to feel inconsiderate if you get a present from someone and then you throw it away. But if you aren't even using the gift, and it is just taking up space in your home, then it really isn't being used in the manner the giver intended. Never hold onto a present just because someone you love gave it to you. If it doesn't bring you joy, you aren't using it, and it is just taking up space and cluttering up your home, then it doesn't matter who gave it to you, it is time to get rid of that item.

- **Have tunnel vision and stay in just one room at a time**: When you get started with decluttering a specific room, don't let yourself fall prey to a bunch of distractions. This can seem pretty simple to remember but there are times when you need to watch the kids, you think of something else that you need to get done that day, or you just can't seem to concentrate. But when you get started with decluttering a room, turn on the tunnel vision and just concentrate on getting that room done. That can help you to stay focused and get the work done faster than if you stop and go as you handle other tasks.

- **Don't overdo it. One room a day is fine**:

Decluttering can take some time to accomplish. It is not a task that you can rush and while it can be done quickly, for the first time, you need to just focus your work on just one room at a time. Once you are done with one room, take it easy and do something else. This helps to take the stress out of the job and can help you to not get burnt out from the process.

- **Find easy ways to get rid of your stuff**: If you make it too difficult to get rid of the items that you have, then you are going to run into trouble. You will separate things out in your home, but then you won't actually get rid of them. These things will stay in your car, or in the closet, or somewhere else in your home and just causes a mess again. Find the method that works the best for you to get that stuff out of your home right away.

- **Maintain the clutter free zone in your home**: To prevent more things coming into your home and causing a mess, it is important to maintain an environment that is clutter free. To do this, make a list of all the things that you absolutely need to have in your home. Whether it is in household goods, appliances, clothes, or something else, know exactly what you need. Anything else is extra and shouldn't make it into your home. Don't waste time browsing through catalogs, going through stores, or looking online, because these are very good at convincing you to make a purchase of something that you don't need. Stick with the basics, the necessities, and you will be able to keep the clutter out of your home.

- **Make decluttering a habit**: Decluttering should not be something you do just once and then never pay attention to again. If you want to make sure that your home stays organized, then decluttering needs to become a regular part of your routine. Make it a habit to declutter once a week, or to get rid of something from your home each day. It is a simple way to keep your home clean and free of clutter.

A decluttering mindset can make a world of difference when it comes to how much stuff you can get rid of, and how clean you can keep your house. If you are too attached to the sentimental things, or if you are too overwhelmed with the work ahead, then you may burn out and not want to keep up with the work. Adopt some of the ideas above, and you will find that it is easier to keep up with decluttering and simplifying your life.

# Chapter 3: Top 10 Reasons Why You Haven't Started Decluttering Already

While decluttering may seem like the perfect solution to your messy house and messy life, there are still tons of people who don't do any sort of decluttering, or they do it on a very rare basis. There are many reasons why people may try to avoid decluttering their homes and lives, but often it has to do with finding too much sentimental value in things, and feeling overwhelmed at all the work that needs to be done with this process.

Some of the top reasons why you, or someone else, may not have already started with decluttering their homes and lives may include:

1. **The memories**: It is pretty common for people to hold onto their favorite

memories through objects, but this is also a reason why they are stuck in the past. Many times, the items that we hold onto are just reminders of a good time in our past or a period of our lives that we want to remember. Always trust that these experiences are going to stay in your heart. If you need to, take a picture of that item and then give the item away if you aren't using it.

2. **They aren't sure how long to keep things**: This can be a big issue in many homes. How do you know it is time to sell, donate, or toss an item if you have no idea how long to keep it in the first place. Some items should be gotten rid of earlier than others, but most of the time, we hold onto items for much longer than we need to.

3. **You don't know how to let go**: Letting go of items, especially ones that you feel are sentimental, can be a big part of the

decluttering process. This can be hard when it comes to letting an item go or not. But you need to learn that these things are just things, and nothing that is important. It is fine to let them go and move on to bigger and better things in your life.

4. **A sense of security**: Certain objects can provide people with a false sense of security. We make ourselves feel like we are comfortable and secure when we acquire things. This could just be the way that the person is wired or it could be something that goes back to childhood.

When going through your home, ask yourself if you really need that item at all. While you don't have to go through and overanalyze how things are, it is still a good idea to stop and think about why you purchase, store, and use things before deciding whether or not to keep that item.

5. **A remorse over a bad purchase**: It is common for people to make a purchase on a whim, and many times this can result in them overspending on the item, and then feeling guilty when the item sits in its original box without being used at all. After spending a lot of money on an item, it can be hard to face the feelings of failure for that bad decision.

   It is fine to feel buyer's remorse sometimes, but this should not be an excuse to hold onto the item. Donate them to someone who may need them. Use this as a learning experience to keep yourself from doing the same things again.

6. **A fear of letting things go**: Another issue that some people may encounter is that they have a fear of letting things go. They may be so attached to their stuff for many different reasons that they are scared of letting it go. It may be a fear of

scarcity or not having enough, which could create a habit of hoarding and stockpiling, or a fear that they will forget the memories, which is why some people may hold onto memorabilia, photos, and artwork.

The best thing that you can do to help this is to address the reasons why you hold onto things and then create a plan that allows you to let go of these things. You may find that it seems a bit silly when you actually say it out loud, and you may then be willing to let the item go.

7. **The idea of decluttering is too overwhelming**: For some people, the reason they don't spend time decluttering is that it is just too much for them to handle. They may feel that it is overwhelming to go through everything in their homes, and then making quick decisions about whether to keep that item

or not. And the idea of doing the physical work to get rid of items can be hard. The best thing to do here is to remember that decluttering doesn't have to happen overnight. It is fine to take a week, a month, or even a few months to declutter your whole home. No one expects you to go through and declutter the whole house overnight.

8. **They don't know where to start**: Most people have larger homes, ones that can hold a lot of stuff, and it is sometimes hard to know where to start. They may walk into a room and wonder what they need to work on first. This can sometimes be bad enough that they then get overwhelmed, and start looking through things and not doing the work at hand.

9. **They don't realize how much clutter is actually in their home**: Some people may be in denial about how much of a

mess they actually have in their homes. They may notice that there is a bit of a mess, but they say things like "I've been busy", "I have kids that make it messy", and so on. What they don't realize is that by decluttering and organizing things in their home, they could actually help to make life easier and require less cleaning.

10. **They don't want to put in the time or effort**: Some people are just too lazy to get the work done. We are all busy and have lots of activities to get to, but there are some people who look at the clutter and just sweep it under the rug. They don't want to deal with it and would rather spend their time doing something else. But with a little bit of time out of your day, you can make a big difference in how clean your home is and how much clutter is found there, saving you time and energy the next time you want to clean or you have trouble finding something you need.

There are many different reasons why people do not want to spend time cleaning up their homes and decluttering their lives. And the reasons above are some of the most common. If you find that you are suffering from some of the reasons above, it is time to make some changes and realize all the good that decluttering can do in your life.

# Chapter 4: Top 10 Benefits of Turning Your Decluttering Into a Habit

Decluttering your home may seem like such a simple process, one that may make your home a bit cleaner, but that is about it. But there are so many benefits that you can get when it comes to decluttering your home. You can free up more of your time, spend less of your time and energy on cleaning the home, and it can even help you to improve your overall health. Some of the benefits that you can enjoy when you pick up a decluttering habit include:

## 1. Keeps your home clean without having to waste the weekend

How many times have you gotten to the weekend, and dreaded it because you knew you would need to spend the whole time or at least a good chunk of it, cleaning up? Many people find that when there is a lot of clutter around the home, they end up spending way too much of their free time trying to keep it all clean and tidy.

If you go through the process of decluttering, you can help get rid of a lot of the stuff that is in your home. This can go a long way when it comes to how much you need to pick up during the weekends. If you are able to keep up on the decluttering during the week and make sure that you don't start going through and purchasing more stuff after the process is done, you will free up more of your weekend to do the things that you want.

For those who are tired of wasting all their free time on the weekends or day off, then decluttering may be the process that you need. It does take some time in the beginning, simply because there is so much clutter and not a lot of organization throughout your home. But once you get these things down, you are going to see a big difference in how quickly you can clean up the home. A few minutes each night should be plenty (once the major decluttering process is done) and you can then spend the rest of your free time doing what you want to do.

## 2. Makes it easier to find what you need

Think about how much time you have wasted in your life trying to find the things that you need? It can be frustrating to look for the keys when it is time to go or to search around for another important thing that you need before starting your day. The more clutter you have, the harder it is to find the items you really need. When you go through the process of decluttering, you can get rid of all the extra and unnecessary things, freeing up more time and space for the things that are actually important. And overall, this will make it much easier for you to find what you need.

How many times have you had to scramble around in the morning to find your keys? How many times have you been frustrated because you couldn't find what you need? How many times have you been late to an appointment or an important meeting, because you spent that time searching for the right thing to wear, or for the document you needed to take with you?

Decluttering can make this whole process so much easier. You will learn that everything has a place, and you will get into the habit of placing them in those places. And when the clutter is gone, it is easier to look around a room and find exactly what you are looking for without all the hassle.

### 3. Less time picking things up

Any time that you clean the house, you spend the majority of that time and effort picking up clutter. Most of the stuff is unnecessary and just in the way, and most of it is waste. You could spend hours cleaning up your home and most of it is stuff that only has the purpose of ending up back on your floor. If you get rid of that clutter, you can spend less time picking up your home and more time doing something that you enjoy.

If you get rid of half the items that are in your home, you could technically get rid of half the time that you usually spend with your cleaning process. The more that you can donate or throw out, the easier it can be for you to clean up the home, and then spend more time doing the things that you really want to do. Even if the process of decluttering your whole home may seem daunting and a little boring, think of all the free time you are going to gain later on.

## 4. It is easier to clean your home without all the clutter in your way

This may seem pretty obvious, but the less stuff you have in your home on the floor or on the counter, the faster you can clean up the home. If you are constantly putting the stuff away just to see it back on the floor, chances are you are dealing with a lot of clutter and it is time to clean it up. Start by going through the whole house and getting rid of anything that you don't use. There are some methods later in this guidebook that can make the process easier, and you can choose the method that you like the best.

Once the clutter is all gone, you get the benefit of having less to pick up during your cleaning schedule. Simply set up a regular cleaning schedule to keep the house looking nice, and avoid bringing in more clutter at the same time, and you are going to find that it only takes a half hour or so to clean up, rather than the whole day.

## 5. There is more time for the people and the things that are important to you

The more that you have, the more that you have to waste your time and energy caring for those things. The less that you have, the more time you can spend on the people and things that are really important for you. It may not seem like a big deal to have a few extra items sitting around the house, but think about how much time you are wasting on those items rather than spending your time with the ones you love or doing the things that you love.

When you go through the decluttering process, ask yourself whether you would rather spend your time taking care of that item, or spend time with your loved ones? You may find that this makes it a whole lot easier to throw out some items that you have been holding onto.

## 6. Some freedom from the scarcity mindset

Many of us are going to do some rationalization when it comes to the items that we convince ourselves to keep. We think that we will use the item later on, or that we may need it at some point. In reality, we don't really need these things at all, we are just focused on a scarcity mindset, or believing that we must hold onto something because we may need it or it can save us money to have that item. Even in a world where there is plenty and no one is starving or constantly looking for food, this scarcity mindset can get us to hold onto things we do not need.

Instead of holding onto those shoes that may look good next spring, but which you haven't worn in three years, or instead of holding onto something "Just in case", it is time to let them go. This can clear up a lot of room in your home and can make life easier.

## 7.  Freedom from holding onto the ideas of the past

Many times we hold onto items because they are about the past. We enjoyed different periods of our lives, times that gave us hope, made us feel good, and were fun. And some of the items that we have can remind us about this time. When an item is tied back to a particular time in our past, it can be even harder to let it go. Instead of hoarding onto that item and letting it take up space in your life, it is much better to let those items go. If they hold a very special place in your heart, take a picture and keep that as proof.

## 8. Being able to live more in the here and now

There is nothing better than being able to live in the here and now. Too many times we focus on what we need to do in the future, or what has happened in the past. When you focus on decluttering your life, you can let go of some of those things that remind you so much about the past and can help you worry less about how much time you will need to spend on cleaning up your home and your life in the future. You can instead focus your time and attention on the things that you like to do now and the things that make you the happiest now.

## 9. Can lead to decluttering in other areas of your life, such as your schedule or your mind

Once you figure out how to declutter your home, you can take these lessons and this practice and put it towards other parts of your life. Imagine how nice it would be to have a decluttered schedule, a decluttered mind, and just a decluttered life? If you are successful with decluttering your home, these other aspects of your life will naturally start to fall into place as well.

## 10. Can help improve your health

Studies have shown how decluttering can actually help to improve your health. There are a number of reasons why this may be true. First, decluttering allows you to have a cleaner home, which is going to make it easier for you to get things done, easier to focus on tasks that you have in front of you, and even easier for you to relax. Many of us don't realize it, but it is really hard to even relax when our homes are messy. With decluttering, you can have an easier time getting your home organized so you can sit back and relax.

Decluttering could also help your health in the fact that you are clearing out some of the attachment that you have to things. Many of us in this consumer world are forming attachments to actual things, like our computers, our phones, pictures, and many other things. We may refuse to declutter our lives because we are slightly attached to them. Being able to let things go can free us up from being so attached to things.

Finally, decluttering can also help reduce your stress levels. Having a home that has a lot of clutter around it can be stressful. Running around trying to find the keys or other things that are needed in the morning can be stressful. All of this can add up to a lot of stress in our lives. Being able to clean out some of the clutter can do wonders for clearing out some of the stress.

# Chapter 5: How to Organize Your Time to Make Decluttering Easier

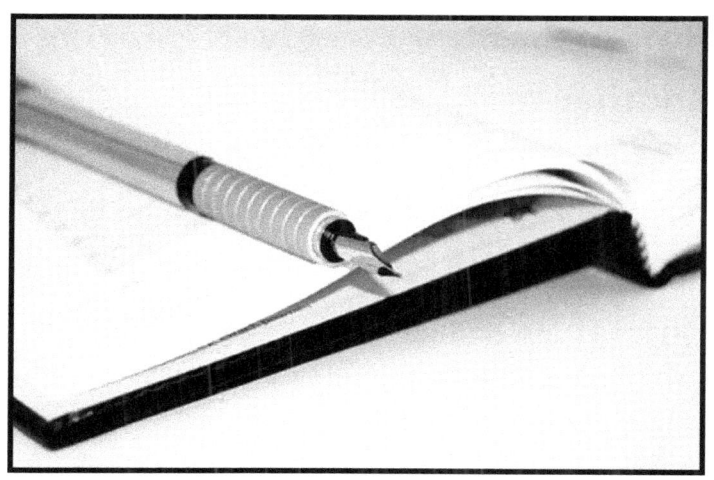

When you are ready to get started with the process of decluttering, it is important that you learn how to properly organize your own time. If you are not organized with a good routine and you don't learn the right management techniques, it is easy to feel overwhelmed, get distracted, or have other issues that come up that make it hard for you to actually get the work done. Let's take a look at some of the steps that you can take to make decluttering easier, and helps you to stay on track in the process.

## How to Create a Weekly Organizing Routine

While we are going to spend some time in this guidebook talking about decluttering, and how you can get started by going through your home, and keeping or getting rid of things that you need or don't need, you can't just do this once and assume it is going to stay that way permanently. Decluttering and organizing is an ongoing process, and teaching yourself how to stay on this schedule can make a big difference in the results that you get.

Your home, as well as your life, needs a lot of upkeep to help it stay organized. This is especially true when it comes to the process of decluttering.

If you don't take the time to declutter on a regular basis, everything is going to pile up and it can become overwhelming. But thinking about organizing your living space can seem daunting.

The best solution that you can stick with is to dedicate a little bit of time every day and then work in 15-minute increments to make this work. You may be surprised at how much you will be able to get done when it comes to decluttering, and organizing any room in your home with just those 15 minutes. Let's take a look at some of the steps that you can take to make this work for you.

First, you should develop your own organizing routine for the week. This routine can be personalized for your needs, but it is meant to help you get through your home, and keep each space decluttered with only spending a few minutes each day. We are going to look at one example, and this one is going to focus a lot on some of the high-traffic areas such as the kitchen, entryway, closet, bedrooms, and bathrooms. You can make the plan as detailed as you would like, but this one is going to include some time for meal planning, meal prep, and laundry as well to make it easier.

Your weekly organization routine is going to include a list of tasks that need to be done each week. You can then pair it with the day that makes the most sense to do this task. Since everyone has a different schedule to follow, your organization routine can be personalized to work with you. But this routine is basically going to be a schedule to keep you on track, with a little bit of flexibility added in so that you can get everything done.

There are a few tools that you can implement into your routine to help you out. You simply need a timer to help you keep track of how much time has passed, a bag or a recycling bin, and a wastebasket and you should be set.

First, there are a few things that you must make sure that you do every day, regardless of what other tasks you have on your list for the week. These things include:

- **First five minutes**: During this time, you can clean off the clutter on the coffee table, bathroom vanity, and kitchen counter. This is a simple sweep that can take all the clutter off and then you put everything back in its place. You can also choose to toss the clutter if it is something that you don't want to keep around.

- **The second five minutes**: Check out your launch pad. This should be the area where you keep important things, such as your incoming and outgoing mail, your cell phone, and keys. You may want to consider having one of these to help you keep some important items in one place so you don't have to search for them all the time.

- **Last five minutes**: This is where you need to clear off the clutter from clothes from rooms where the clothing doesn't belong. This would include clearing the clothes from places like the kitchen, the living room, and the bathroom. You can either put this back into the bedroom or the laundry room until you get to cleaning it.

For the next fifteen minutes or so, it is time to really declutter the room that you have chosen for the day, or do the other task that needs to be done. Some people decide to spend that time quickly going through the rooms of the house, or they will divide up the tasks that need to be done into each day. One day you may clean out the sink or the stove, one you clean the toilets in the bathroom, and another where you fold the laundry. You can set up the schedule that works the best for you.

A routine can be the best thing to help you stay on track when it comes to keeping your decluttering in check. This helps you to make this a habit that you are used to, and can ensure that you get everything cleaned. And it only needs to take fifteen minutes or so a day to see success. Think of all the free time you will have on the weekends if you can keep up with the routine that you set!

## Management Tips When Decluttering Your Home

The amount of clutter that you can accumulate in your home can be amazing. Many of us just move it around our homes, making promises that we will get rid of it at some point, but then just moving it around again. It is amazing how much clutter can get into the home and how much of our time is spent dealing with that clutter.

The hardest part about getting started with decluttering is figuring out how to get started. We may look at the process of decluttering our homes and our lives, and then worry that it is such a big task and we will never be able to get it all done. Being able to manage our time and coming up with a plan to tackle it all in a timely manner will help solve this issue. Some of the management tips that you can use when it comes to decluttering your home include:

- **Make a list**: Much like how you would sit down and come up with a grocery list before you go shopping, you should sit down and make a list for each room of what you absolutely need to keep there. This list is going to help you keep on track when you get to work. You can get a good feeling any time that you check something off the list. Now, you may not be able to think of all the items in each room that has to stay, but it helps you have a good idea of what needs to stay and what should go.

- **Go through one room at a time**: Even if you start out with a ton of motivation at the beginning, there is no way you can go through this whole process in one day. This is overwhelming and there is just too much to get done. Instead, just go into one room and make it your goal to get it done. You may be able to get a few rooms done in a day if you get going, but you should not make it your goal to get the entire home done. When you select just one or two at a time, this can help you focus on that space and it just makes your decluttering process easier.

- **Set your time limit**: Have you ever gotten into decluttering and then find that you get distracted looking through an old yearbook or something else that you haven't looked at for a long time? This can be a fun process, but it is not a good idea if you are trying to clean up your home. Before you even take a look at a particular room, set a time limit to get the work done. Twenty to thirty minutes is often plenty to help you get the room done and stay on task.

- **Seasonize**: What this means is that you can organize your items based on the season that you are most likely to use them. You can use some space bags to hide away your sweater in the summer, and some boxes to put away the Christmas decorations. This helps you to keep some of those items that you use during certain times of the year while still decluttering your home at the same time.

- **Get rid of items**: There are several different methods that you can use to get rid of items. You can donate them, you can give them away to friends, or you can try to sell these at a garage sale or online. You can pick any of these options, but make sure that you go through and get rid of those items, rather than letting them sit in a corner for months on end. It doesn't do you a lot of good if your unused and unwanted items just sit there while still being in your home. Get rid of them within a few days after you do the decluttering to help get them out of the home.

- **Make use of the space that you have**: If you look around your home, you are likely to have space that you could use already. Clean out a junk drawer, use a closet after it is cleaned out, or some other space to help you to get the most storage possible in the space that you have.

# Chapter 6: How to Set Your Priorities When Housekeeping and How to Create a Plan

Now that you have gotten the basics of decluttering, you are ready to jump in and see what else you can accomplish if you set your mind to it. Decluttering is a process that can take some time, but the rewards are definitely worth it. Here, we are going to take some time to create a simple decluttering plan so you can get to work, and ensure that your home will be easier to keep clean and that the clutter is finally gone.

## Before

There are a few different things that you will need to do before you decide to get started with the decluttering process. Some of the steps that can help you begin include:

- **Write down the date in your calendar**: Yes, you must write it down. It is not enough for you to just say it in your head, you need to write it down to make things official. Set about 30 to 60 minutes for each room in your home. If you plan to do a few rooms, then go ahead and write them both down during the same day. You need to treat these just like any other appointment that you need to handle, so pick a day when you can be free and can devote your whole attention to getting it done.

- **Find someone to help you get it done**: You can either hire someone to be your assistant through this process or find others in your family to help. Having that second pair of hands can keep you company and can make it easier to get through the process. This other person can also help you to stick with your goals and will hold you accountable. It even makes it easier for you to part with some of the items that you may have kept.

- **Have some cleaning products nearby**: You will need to clean as you go to get the most benefits out of this. So grab some cleaning solution, some rags, a dustpan, and a broom to help you get going.

- **Have your lunch (and even supper) prepared ahead of time**: Once you get going with the decluttering, you are going to get focused and trying to get things done. When you finish, or maybe even sometime in the process of cleaning, you will start to feel hungry and want to eat. Having lunch prepared, whether you throw something into the slow cooker, go to a local café, or eat some leftovers, can help you so much once your brain is tired from all the work.

- **Gather up the old boxes and bags that you have**: The bags can be great for gathering up the things that you want to give away as donations. For your time in the kitchen, you may need some newspapers and cardboard boxes to deal with some of the more fragile items.

## During

Now that we know a bit about what is needed during the before period, it is time to be prepared for when you actually start to go through the process of decluttering. First, you should begin your decluttering process going category by category. If you do set aside the whole day, then have the goal for that day be tackling the whole wardrobe. If you only have time to do an hour or so of decluttering, then you can pick out some kind of sub-category to help you complete the work in the allotted time.

For example, let's say you only have 30 minutes to devote to this process in one day. You could start by tackling all the jackets in the closet on that day. Grab all the jackets from wherever they may be hiding in the home and put them away nicely. If there is still time, then you could move on the second category, such as cleaning up your shoes. Aim to get as many of these subcategories done in your allotted time.

Now you can work on staging your belongings. Simply by taking all the items and removing them from where you hide them in your home, you are faced with the total volume of all that you own. This can be a kind of shock factor because you may have never realized how many shoes or other items you have at your disposal. This sometimes makes it easier for you to get rid of some of the items. And when you compare some of your older items to some of the newer ones, it is easier to help you throw some of the older ones out. Stage your items first, and then you can go through and make decisions about what you want to keep and what you want to throw out.

## After

After you have sorted through all of the items in a particular room, or after you have finished with the decluttering session, there are still a few steps left for you to accomplish. Doing these before you call it quits, can help you to get all those unwanted and unneeded items out of your home, and can provide you with the freedom that you need. Some of the steps that you can take to finish up your decluttering session include:

- **Wrap up the loose ends**: Aim to leave a bit of time at the end of your cleaning session to drop off donations if you can. This may need a bit of extra energy, but doing it right away will ensure those items get dropped off, and that they don't just sit around your home for a long time to come.

- **Recoup some cash if you can**: Depending on the items that you plan to get rid of, you may be able to sell some of them and make some extra money. You may decide to have a garage sale or sell some of the items online and make a few extra bucks. Use this to help pay down some of your debt or to do something fun, but never use that money to go out and purchase more material possessions, or you may be going against all the hard work that you have just done.

The process of decluttering is not meant to be really difficult. Instead, it is meant as a way to make your life easier and less stressful. Setting up a plan and moving from one room to another can really make a difference in how much you can get done, and how overwhelming the whole process can be.

# Chapter 7: The Steps You Need to Declutter the Kitchen

The first room we are going to take a look at is the kitchen. This is a room that gets a lot of traffic from the family. Not only do we spend time cooking and eating meals in there, but many times it is the place to entertain guests, to work on homework with the kitchen table, and even pay bills and more.

Since the kitchen is such a high traffic area, it can be hard to keep it clutter free and looking nice. This chapter is going to spend some time discussing the simple steps, that you can take in order to help get that kitchen cleaned and spotless and to keep it that way.

## Simple Steps to Help You Declutter the Kitchen Quickly

Take a quick look at your kitchen. This is the area where you and your family will dump a lot of stuff, including food, backpacks, mail, and so much more. It is likely that the countertops are crammed with fruit that you need to have eaten, a lot of electronics that are being charged, and even extra appliances, most of which are never used.

This kitchen area can easily get crammed with a lot of stuff, which makes the idea of decluttering feel like a big task. But there are some steps that you can take to help make this process easier. The steps you need for cleaning up the kitchen include:

## *Set a timer*

For most people, it is hard to declutter the whole kitchen in one day. This can be overwhelming and can wear you out quickly. If you are able to do this, then go ahead, but for most people, breaking it up over a few days and doing 30 minutes at a time is a much better option and can keep fatigue at bay. Before you decide to start, go and gather several boxes. You should have a box for relocating, one for items you want to sell, and one for items to donate. You may also need to bring some recycling bags and garbage bags to help with disposal.

When you are ready to start, turn on the time and have it run for the next 30 minutes. Spend your time focusing just on the kitchen and all that you can get done as the time counts down. You can decide at the end whether you would like to go for longer or not.

## *Focus on just one area at a time*

It may seem easy to open up random cabinets in the home and start working, but this can create a lot of chaos and clutter. The best strategy is to open just one cabinet or one drawer. Then go through each item there and figure out whether you would like to keep it or get rid of it. Keep going through this process until that whole drawer or cabinet is taken care of. Make sure that you don't graze through the kitchen and declutter at random though. Take the time to do one area at a time to efficiently clean the kitchen.

## *Question all of the items you pick up*

As you work through the kitchen and are sorting through items, there are a few questions that you should ask yourself including:

- Do I use this?
- How many do I have of this item?
- Would I purchase this item to use today if I saw it at the store?

Be honest with yourself when asking these questions, and don't let the price of something convince you to keep an item that you never use. If you don't actually use that tool or that appliance, then it is just taking up some valuable room, and it is time to get it gone. If you are worried about how much the item originally cost, consider selling it online or at a garage sale to recover some of that lost money.

## *Remove anything out of the room that doesn't belong there*

As you go through the kitchen, you may notice that there are quite a few things that are there that don't really belong. You may see some toys, some clothes, some shoes, some backpacks, old mail, and more. This is a room that seems to catch a lot of the random stuff of the home that should be put elsewhere. This is the step where you take all those items and place them in their proper location in the house.

Kitchen countertops are known for being a big dumping ground for everyone in your home. Grab these items and start putting them away where they belong. If you are in a hurry to get the decluttering done, bring in a box and throw all the stuff that needs to be relocated into this box to deal with later. This still helps you to get that stuff off the counter and out of your way for now.

**Set yourself up to reach success.**

Even the most simplified kitchen isn't going to be able to stay that way if you don't maintain it on a regular basis. This is why you need to implement a system that can help catch all the clutter that comes in, and there will be clutter over time.

To start with this, look and see what you and other members of your family do in the kitchen. Sure, you spend time cooking and eating in that room, but what other things happen in that room? Do you use it to pay your bills and look up some recipes? Do your kids do some of their homework there as you make supper? The system that you create needs to be able to accommodate all of the tasks that are completed in that room.

For example, if you like to pay bills in the kitchen, then you can dedicate a basket or a bin to store the mail until you can get to it later. If your kids like to spend time doing homework in the room, then dedicate some space to make this easier for them. Keep notebooks, pens, and pencils in a cabinet or a drawer that is out of the way and can hold onto all these items.

# Some Easy Tips to Help You Organize the Kitchen

Organizing the kitchen may take a little time, but there are some steps that you can take to ensure that it won't take a week to accomplish. With a few little tricks, you will be able to turn your kitchen into a clean area, one where you can easily find everything that you need in just a few seconds. Some of the tips that you can follow when it comes to decluttering your kitchen include:

- **Create some mini-stations**: This is a good method to go with because it ensures that all similar items stay in one common area. An example of this is if you like to drink coffee. You would then make a refreshment station on a side with everything that is needed to make the coffee. This makes it easier for everyone to be in one place and ensures you won't make a mess of the kitchen in the process.

- **Invest in some baskets**: Baskets can be so nice when it comes to your kitchen. These are great for decluttering the kitchen in a manner that is smart and attractive. You can store any item in them that you want before adding to a cabinet, or you can use hanging baskets to give you more space. They are also really easy to access any time that you want to get an item out of them.

- **Get rid of appliances that you don't use**: This doesn't mean you have to get rid of all your appliances and if you are still using one, then don't get rid of it. But if you have an item that you never use, then they just take up space. If you haven't used one of the items in the last three months in your kitchen, then it is time to donate it or throw it away.

- **Hang up some things**: If you have space and seem to be out of cupboard space way before you think you should, consider hanging up your pans and your pots. This can save some of the space on your shelves and makes the items easier to access, clean, and reuse. You can hang them up on a wall, on the pantry door, or the back of cabinets. There are many no damage hooks or cup holder screws that can help make this easier.

- **Put that lazy space in the kitchen to work**: It is pretty common to waste a lot of space in the kitchen without even realizing it. For example, the space between the cabinet and the ceiling can be put to work for you just like anywhere else. You could construct your cabinet all the way to the ceiling to fix this problem or invest in some storage baskets that can go up there to save your budget and some time.

- **Organize all the shelves**: To do this, you will need to take some time to rearrange things. You can add in some shelves for dinner food, for cereal, and even for some paper products. While working on your shelves, make sure that every item has its own zone so that no matter who comes into your kitchen, they will be able to find the thing they are looking for.

- **Give lids a home**: No one likes to deal with the lids. While we do need them for storage purposes, they often take up a lot of room and just don't seem to fit anywhere nicely. The best way to take care of those lids is to store the lids for your pans and pots separately, to make it easier to access them when you need them most. You can use any space that you want, such as your pantry, a cabinet, or give them their own drawer, just don't store them directly with the pot or pan they go on.

- **Put the items where you are most likely to use them**: You can also divide up your kitchen into specific zones. You should have things like cutting boards, mixing bowls, and other food preparation tools near the largest workspace available in the kitchen. But those items that help with cooking, such as bakeware, pans, potholders, and more, should be near the stove. Then your serving supplies, like napkins, flatware, and dishes, can be near the dining room. Things like foil, Tupperware, and other storage containers do well near the refrigerator and towels, trash bags, and cleaning supplies can work well near the dishwasher. This helps you to put everything in its place and can make it all easily accessible when you need it most.

- **Use the back of pantry and cabinet doors**: Another tip that you can follow when it comes to decluttering your home is to use some clear hanging shoe organizers in your pantry to store a few things. Add it to the back of your pantry door and then hold a ton of items in it such as straws, toothpicks, recipe cards, and more. You can also trim down the organizer if it happens to be too big or wide for what you want to use it for.

## Maintaining the Kitchen Clean

After you have put in all of the work above, it is important that you don't let the place become a mess again. It is so easy to do the work and then never touch it again. But if you don't do upkeep in the kitchen, you are going to end up with a room that is messy and cluttered all over again.

Each day, spend about ten minutes in the kitchen. Wipe down the counters after you cook, and wash all of your dishes after every meal. Do a quick sweep through the kitchen at the end of the day, and mop if you feel the floor needs it. Once a month, go through and clean out the fridge and the cupboards, getting rid of any food that may have passed its expiration date, or anything that may be old or you won't use any longer.

Cleaning your kitchen can take up some time. We often throw a lot of knick-knacks in this area and it is hard to sort through everything. Add in that there is so much to sort through between the pantry, the fridge, and all the cupboards, and it can be a big area to work on. But having a plan and dedicating some time to get it done can make all the difference in how much decluttering you get done.

# Chapter 8: Decluttering the Common Living Space

After you have time to work on the kitchen, it is time to move on to the second room in the home — the living room. This is a place where your family gathers to spend time together. It is a place where you can share a lot of memories. It is also a place that a lot of people are going to see first when they come into your home. Making sure that it is neat and tidy can make a big difference in how people perceive your home, and how messy the rest of the home is.

Since you and your family spend so much time in the living room, it is not surprising that so much clutter can accumulate there. Being able to handle the clutter and getting rid of everything that is just in the way can make a big difference. Let's look at some of the steps that you can take to help declutter your living room and make it feel more comfortable and inviting.

## How to Declutter the Living Room

When you are ready to clean out your living room, there are a few things that you can do to make the process easier. First, you will want to begin with dusting. You can either get some good dusting spray and a cloth to wipe down everything, or invest in a vacuum that can help do this as well. Go through and dust off everything in that area to make it look a bit nicer. Clean off the tables and end tables as you go and either throw things away or put them where they belong, such as a newspaper stand for all your magazines and books.

Next, take a look at the shoes that are in the way. It is best if you and your family members get into the habit of taking your shoes off before you enter the home. But in some cases, this doesn't happen. Clear the shoes out of the room and put these items in their own personal spot in the home. Take a look at how many shoes are in your living room as well. If one pair keeps being brought out but is never really worn, it may be time to throw it away.

Paper paraphernalia can really take over the living room as well. Newspapers, magazines, school work, mail, and more can be everywhere. Go through and pick all of this up off the floor and get rid of anything that you don't need right then and there. You can then pick up any books that are on the floor, as well as any magazines and other similar items that are in the way.

And now, it is time to deal with the clutter in your living room. Take a moment to think of some of the places in your living room that tends to accumulate a lot of clutter. The coffee table can be to blame, end tables, shelves, and more. Clear off the clutter at this time to help you get rid of anything that is in the way there. Decide whether you want to keep the item or not, and then place it where you want it to stay.

Take another look around the room and determine what else needs to be handled. If there are still items that are in the way, then you need to decide if you want to keep them or not. If you decide to keep them, then find a place for those items right away. If you don't want to keep those items, then now is the time to get rid of them.

After you have had time to clean up all the mess on the floor and in the rest of the home, it is time to vacuum. Take your time with this and get all the dust and junk off the floor. This process should be done at least once or twice a week to help maintain the decluttering that you have done, and to help keep the carpet in good working order. If you have time, and a few times a year as well, consider doing a carpet clean as well to really finish up the room.

## The Four Looks Decluttering Method

Now it is time to get into the basics of decluttering your living room. To start, take a look around the room and see what things are obviously trash (such as wrappers, tissues, and so on) that you need to throw away from the beginning. A good approach is to start in one corner and then slowly move through the room. After you pick up all the trash on the floor, you can look through the room again and see which items that look like clutter, and which you want to get rid of right now. This isn't something to overthink. Just go for the things that you know for sure are clutter right off the bat and then get rid of those particular items.

The first two passes should be pretty quick but can clean up a lot of the room at the same time. Now you can look for the third time, and see what items are in the room that doesn't belong there, and needs to put somewhere else in the home. This may be shoes, hair brushes, and so on. Take your time to pick these things up. You can either go and put them away right this second, or you can place them in a box to deal with when you are all done.

At this point, do a fourth look through and see what is still left in that room. Does everything fit there and look like it belongs, or is there still a cramped feeling in the room? If you still feel like there is too much stuff in that space, then it is time to make the hard decisions and you must really go through and decide what can stay and what goes. Be serious with yourself in determining what you would like to keep so that room becomes less cluttered.

After this time, the living room should be picked up and more organized. You should have everything put where it belongs, in other parts of the home or in that room, and you should have gotten rid of all the items that needed to be thrown away. When you look around the living room, you should notice that there is more room to breathe and it doesn't feel as cluttered any longer.

## Tips to Help You Get Even More Out of Your Living Room

- **Dare to be spare**: With too much furniture, even a living room that is big can look very cramped and crowded. Ease out some of that congestion by keeping things basic. You really only need a few items like a coffee table, an end table, a chair, a bookshelf, and a sofa. If you have a television, get a simple stand for it or consider doing a wall hookup to save even more room.

- **Get rid of all the pileup**: Many people subscribe to some magazine or another, and then they hold onto the past issues of that magazine. This can create a big pileup in your home that is hard to handle. You need to become ruthless with this pileup because all it is doing is taking up your space. Save only the last two issues, or even just one issue of a magazine. If you have an article you want to save, tear it out of the magazine and store in a binder for later.

- **Keep the room clean**: You need to keep the living room maintained, or it won't be long before you are back in the same situation you had when you started. A good rule to remember is that you should always be able to see a minimum of 75 percent of your coffee table.

- **Control the remotes**: If you have a few remotes in your home, group them all together in a decorative bowl or a lidded box. This keeps them from making a mess all over your living room and can make it easier for you to find them later.

- **Cut out some of the pillows**: You do not need to have fifty pillows in your living room. This takes up a lot of space and can make it difficult to keep the area clean. A trio in complementary patterns and colors, with one being solid, can be just fine for most sofas. You may want to consider cutting all pillows out to save clutter and room.

- **Double up**: Make sure that you are maximizing storage and get some extra seating at the same time. Use an ottoman to help you hide stuff inside. This allows you to store pillows, blankets, and more, while still having an extra spot to sit in your living room.

- **Floor show**: Having too many area rugs has a way of chopping up the room visually. Instead, you can consider layering a statement rug over carpeting or over your bare floors.

- **Rule of three**: When you are working on what to put away on a shelf, restrict any items that are not books to only three per each shelf. The shapes and sizes can vary, but try to relate them by theme or color to make the area look nicer.

- **Lighten up your library**: Yes, you may love to read, but this doesn't mean you need to hang on to each book you have ever read. Try to reduce your library as much as you can, and consider moving some onto your e-reader to get the best results.

Your living room is an area that lots of people in the family gather and spend time together in, and it is often a room that a lot of people are going to notice when they come to see your home. Make sure that you take the time to declutter your living room, and get it to look nice with the help of the tips that we listed above!

# Chapter 9: The Dreaded Bathrooms and How to Make Them More Manageable

The bathroom is one area of the home that most people do not want to spend their time cleaning. This room often has a lot of different items that are all over the place, and cleaning it up can take a lot of time and elbow grease. But it is possible to clean up the bathroom as well and make it more manageable than before. This chapter is going to take a look at some of the things that you can do to help clean up and declutter your bathroom to save a lot of time when getting ready in the morning.

## The ABC's of bathroom storage

When it comes to your bathroom, there are a lot of little things that you need to worry about storing. And many of them are used on a semi-regular basis. You may not need them all the time, but you need them often enough that you don't want to get rid of them at all. This is where the ABC of storage can come into play and help you see some great results. It allows you to sort things out based on how much you use them, and it also keeps the bathroom as organized as possible. The way that you follow this method includes:

"A" storage areas are the ones that are active, easy to access, and hold onto items that are meant to be used all the time, or on a daily basis. When we are in the bathroom, this could include things like the shampoo bottle, the razor, a blow dryer, and the toothbrush. The areas that fit here should be really user-friendly and you want to be able to reach them without any hidden hazards. The mesh bucket in the shower, the top drawer of your sink, or the countertop can all be great places to store these items.

"B" storage areas are going to hold onto items that you may not use each day, but you use weekly or monthly. This area could include some things like nail care equipment, scrunchies, beard trimming kit, and so on. You want these to still be pretty easy to access, but they don't need to be on the top shelf or anything. Places that would count here include above the toilet storage, a cupboard, under the sink, or even in the middle drawer.

Then there are the "C" storage areas. These are going to require more stretching, standing, and bending to get the item. These are things like your fancy makeup, the hot foot massage machine, and other things that you use occasionally, but not necessarily on a regular basis. If you use the item more than two times a year, but fewer than once a month, then it fits in this category. These are going to be put in the places that you don't spend much time in, but somewhere that you can still access when you need them

Now, when you are ready to go through the items that you have in the bathroom, bring along a box as well. Not only will you go through and sort out all your items into the three categories that we talked about above, as well as throwing some of them away. Be careful about the items that you decide to keep and which ones you actually need to throw away.

Trash bags can be useful as well. Take everything that is in your bathroom out of the drawers and cupboards and everywhere else. Then slowly go through and throw things into the different containers. Choose what you want to keep, separating out into A, B, and C, what you want to get rid of, and what you want to store in another location, such as in a hall closet.

Everything should have a place when you are done and everything should be back in place. This is not a room to hold things off as undecided because there often isn't a lot of room around to store these things. Make a decision about the things that you use, and the things that you don't, and then put them all away in the right spot.

With all the items that go into the bathroom, it is sometimes tempting to say that you use an item and need to keep it. But remember that the amount of space that you have in your bathroom is pretty limited, even with adding in some storage, and you don't need to keep everything. In most cases, you could probably be just fine with the A category items and maybe a few B, and then throwing everything else away. At a minimum, make sure you go through your bathroom and get rid of anything that you haven't used in at least the last year. You will be surprised at how much the clutter will go away when you do this.

When you are all done sorting through the items in your bathroom and making it look better, take some time to clean things off. Get those cleaning supplies ready and clean off the counter, the floor, the shower, and the toilet, and everywhere else that needs some attention in your bathroom. Then close the door feeling good that you did a great job making the area look nice.

## Some Tips to Make Decluttering Your Bathroom Easier

The bathroom is a room that most people don't want to deal with. It can be messy, and if you go a long time without picking up, it may be a bit disgusting. If you take the time to declutter the room, you will find that it doesn't take so much time to keep the bathroom clean afterward. Some of the things that you can consider doing in order to help declutter the bathroom, and keep it organized for the long term include:

- **Work on the medicine cabinet**: Get rid of any containers that are empty, or any that contain medicines that are old and outdated. Check to see which medications are ones you don't even use anymore and throw those out as well.

- **Only keep the things you use daily in the bathroom**: Things like the hairbrush and toothbrush can stay in the bathroom. But while a first-aid supply kit is important, it is just taking up space in the bathroom since you don't use it on a regular basis. Find a new home for this kind of stuff.

- **Store the straighteners and hair dryers in a file organizer**: If you use a lot of things to help get your hair ready in the morning, you know how much room their cords can take up. Take a magazine rack or file organizer and attach it to the side of the bathroom sink, or even on the inside of your cabinet door.

- **Consider a magnetic strip**: This magnetic strip can help you hold onto your nail filer, nail clippers, bobby pins, and tweezers. Instead of searching around all the time to find these, attach a magnetic strip inside your medicine cabinet and add all these items there.

- **Use Mason jars to store brushes and toothbrushes**: This can be a great way to make sure that you get everything stored without having them roll around and cause a mess. Plus, you can easily choose from different options and even colors in order to get the look that you want.

- **Add a shelf above the door**: Many bathrooms are short on storage space. But this doesn't mean you can't add in a little bit of your own. Adding in a shelf above the bathroom door, an area you aren't using anyway could be the perfect way to get the results that you want. It doesn't have to be a very big one, just big enough to store a few extra items.

- **Consider using a tray organizer**: A tray organizer, like what you see with your forks, spoons, and other utensils, can also work when it comes to organizing your bathroom. You can add in your toothbrushes, makeup brushes, and more to this organizer, making it easier for you to see where everything is, without worrying about them rolling all over the place.

- **Use a tension rod to hold onto the cleaning**

**products**: Go under your sink and add in a little tension rod. This can be fitted to the size that you need and is a great way to put your cleaning products under the sink without them being in the way or worrying about them falling over. Then, when it is time to clean the mirror, the counters, the toilet, or the floor, you can just reach under the sink and get exactly what you need.

- **Attach a nice spice rack to one of the bathroom walls**: Think about some of those spice racks that you already have in your kitchen. These are a nice way to get those spices off the bottom of your cabinets and can free up so much space. The same can be said when you use them in your bathroom. Attach one to a wall that makes the most sense in your bathroom and store a few things on it.

These are just a few of the different options that you can use in order to free up some space in your bathroom and can help you get that area as organized as possible. The bathroom can be a really hard area to clean up because it is often smaller, and still has to hold onto a lot of different items. When you figure out how to properly store some of those items and you find ways to add in some more storage, you are going to see some great results in how organized your bathroom is.

Remember that when you are done with cleaning up the bathroom, take some time to set up a maintenance schedule to keep the bathroom as clean as possible. Make sure that you wipe all the counters down, clean the toilet, and do a quick clean of the floor as well. A little maintenance on a daily basis can make it easier for you to get some great results when it comes to your bathroom and can make this room a little less of a chore.

# Chapter 10: Cleaning Up the Bedrooms

Do your bedrooms often feel cluttered and like there is a ton of stuff hanging around all the time, things that you have to walk around and push out of the way just to get to bed? If so, one of the best things that you can do is declutter the room and get rid of things that are just in your way. When you remove all the clutter, the room is going to feel spacious and open, and you will have a much better chance of feeling relaxed.

A bedroom is going to be a catchall many times. When you are cleaning the other rooms of the home, you may inadvertently put a lot of random things in your room and then forget they are there. Instead of dealing with the problem, you will keep pushing things around until the room is a mess. You may need to take some time to deal with the mess in your bedroom, so set aside a few days to get it done. Let's take a look at some of the things that you can do to help declutter the bedrooms in your home.

## Getting Rid of the Extra Things that are in your Room

The first step that you should take is to grab a trash bag and then go through your whole room. You are going to need at least a few to keep track of all the different trash and garbage that is there. Start with the trash that is lying around on the floor and taking up space, and then move on to items that may be broken, or ruined linens and clothes. If you are not sure whether you want to throw an item away, then create a 'maybe pile' to go through later on.

Next, you need to focus on anything that doesn't belong. You can then spend the next ten minutes or so going through the bedroom and getting rid of anything that shouldn't be in your room. Look for things like loose change, paperwork, and dishes. Clear out the areas that are even out of sight, like in between the furniture and under the bed.

The best thing that you can do here is to remove these completely out of the bedroom. You can set up a pile that is out of the room for any trash or miscellaneous belongings. Then you can take those items and place them in the right spot when you are ready so you don't end up adding clutter in a different room.

- Now you can take some time to go through your drawers. Take out a drawer and remove all of the items that are inside. Go through each drawer one at a time. Then make up three piles with the things that are in each drawer. Have a pile for garbage, one for donate, and one for things you want to keep. Once you get one drawer done, put all of the "keep" items back inside. Continue this process for every drawer you do.

- When this process is done, you can move the garbage items to the trash. Place the pile to donate in a bag and have it ready to take out soon. You can also offer any items that you want to get rid of to others you know.

- If you are in doubt about an item, then throw it away and free up some room. It is fine to hold onto a few sentimental items if you want, but be careful about holding onto too many items.

- Set up a drawer or space in the room for any of the sentimental objects that you want to keep. This could include items like clothes, ticket stubs, drawings, and letters.

- Decide if the sentimental thing is worth your time to keep it or not. It may have some good memories, but if you have something else that will remind you of that event, or that memory isn't that important for you, then it is time to get rid of the item.

Now you can work on clearing off all the surfaces. Go through the end tables, dresser, and more, and get rid of all the belongings that are just lying around. Throw away anything that you don't want to keep anymore and the only things that you really want to keep in your room should be things like a computer, a lamp, or other types of décor. When everything is put back in place and you get rid of the things you no longer need, it is time to clean off the area. Dust and wipe off anything that needs it.

You can now work on sorting through the clothes that you have. You can work on your wardrobe and decide which items you would like to keep. Take everything out of the dresser and the closet and then sort it all out. You can sort through what you want to donate, what you want to throw out, and what you want to keep. Then you can organize the clothes based on whether they need to go back into the closet or the dresser to make them easier to access.

After everything has been thrown out or ready to donate or put back away, it is time to organize your room. Consider if you want to rearrange the room at all and move the furniture so that it makes the most sense. Even if you don't want to permanently change up the room, it may be a good idea to move things a bit so that you can clean and vacuum under it to make it look nice. We will talk about cleaning the closet later on, but you may want to reorganize this part as well to make it easier to find things.

Another idea is to install shelves. Shelves are a great way to help you add a bit of extra storage so you can keep some of the clutter from the floor. You can go to a hardware store and find some shelving holders that are easy to mount to the bedroom wall, so they don't take up any more space than necessary in your room. Make sure that the shelves are placed high off the ground so you don't have to worry about running into them.

Another option to consider is to use storage furniture. There are plenty of options for furniture that can act as a storage unit. These are helpful if you are limited in closet space and you want to be able to fit linens and other supplies. You can find a lot of options such as a bed frame that has some drawers under the bed, a dresser, and more.

# Keeping Up with the Maintenance of the Cleaning

An important thing to remember when you get started on this process is that you need to maintain the clutter-free zone. It won't do you a lot of good to just start throwing things back on the floor right after you are done. You need to spend a bit of time each day, maybe even just five minutes, cleaning up the bedroom to make it look nice.

The first step is to make sure that your laundry gets put away after it is done. A common way for some of the clutter to build up again is after you are done with laundry. Many people will just shove it into their room and forget about it. Instead of doing this, you can fold the laundry right when it is done and then put it away immediately. Never let piles of clothing build up in your room. If you find that you don't have enough room for these clothes, then it is time to go through them again and get rid of a few things.

If you need some storage for items that are more seasonal, then you can get a storage bin and place it in the attic, the garage, or under the bed.

Take the time to clean up the room on a regular basis as well. Rather than cleaning your room just once a year, take the time to do small bits of cleaning or organizing every day of the week. If you have a bit of clutter in the corner of the room or on the desk, then take the time to clean it up. Never let a small mess accumulate into a big one. You can save yourself a lot of hassle in the future by tackling a little bit of clutter as it forms. You should plan to vacuum or sweep the room at least one time a week.

And finally, you need to make sure that you avoid overbuying anything in the future. It doesn't do you a lot of good to clear out the clutter in your room and then going back out and purchasing a ton of stuff all over again. Hoarding materials and purchasing an impulse buy can make this different. It is time to limit how many belongings you are allowed to purchase.

The next time that you consider going out and purchasing something, take a few minutes to think about where you would put that item in your room. You may think about the stuff that you already have and decide that it is not a good thing to purchase. And if you are considering that it is time to upgrade a belonging, then you should decide whether or not you are willing to get rid of the original of that item.

Cleaning your bedroom can sometimes be the most difficult, because you may keep a lot of personal touches around the room, and a lot of sentimental items there. This can take some time to go through everything and figure out what you would like to keep and what to get rid of. It is fine to keep a few of the decorations around your room, a few pictures, and maybe a few sentimental items. But you need to make sure that you actually have room for them, and that they don't become unnecessary clutter in your room.

# Chapter 11: Watch Out for Those Lego! – How to Declutter Your Kids' Rooms

In addition to cleaning out your other bedrooms, you will also want to take time to clean out the rooms that your kids play in. These rooms will need some special attention to help keep them clean, and it may be a good idea to involve your child in doing some of the work. This ensures that they understand the process that is going on, and will be willing to help out and keep the room clean. Some of the things that you can do when it comes to cleaning your kids' bedroom will include:

**Get your kids involved with the process from the beginning.**

It is not a good idea to just walk into your child's room and start throwing things away. You need to involve them in the process and work with them before you go through and re-organize the room. Kids as young as three want to participate and some can even find it exciting to be involved in this way. You may worry that a child is going to be frustrated or bored when you talk about decluttering a room, but they see it as a way that they can talk about their toys and get attention from their parents.

In addition, when you get your child involved in the organizing process, they are going to be more willing to let you get the work done. They will feel like they have some ownership on the project, and they are more likely to keep things in order when things are done.

## Ask your kid to give you a tour before you start

Never just walk into your child's room and start throwing things away or getting rid of them. It is best to take it slowly and let your child feel like they are the ones in control. Consider starting with letting your child show you what is in their room. This gives you a sense of the tone and language the child will use towards certain things and can give you a good idea of what that child finds the most important.

Really listen to what the child tells you and try to mimic back some of the behavior if you can. This makes it easier for them to trust that you are on their side and that you aren't there just to take their stuff away. Remember that even though these toys are just items, your child has personified them a bit and may feel a connection with them. This is not a bad thing. They don't have the same kind of connection that adults give to items. Listening to your child and figuring out what is valuable to them and how they are feeling at the time can help you be more successful with this endeavor.

**Discuss how all the stuff in the room must have a home.**

Kids are a bit different than adults in that they have a great ability to personify the things around them. So, one method that you can use is asking your child "Where should we give this a home?" when you work on organizing with them. Many times we get caught up in the idea of saying that it is time to put one item or another away, and this can feel very negative to a child. Instead, you could say something like "Can we put that where it lives?" It is a simple change that actually makes a world of difference to a child.

## Give permission for the kid to let go of anything they don't want or use.

Sometimes, the volume, or the amount of stuff in the room, can be overwhelming for your child. But many kids don't know that it is just fine to say no to things they no longer want. They may be worried that they are doing something bad by throwing out or getting rid of the items. Give your child permission to let go of items they don't want, no matter what that item may be. Consider helping them to donate the items to a charity so there is more positivity that comes with letting go of items.

## Start from the bottom up

Another thing to consider is where to start. And with younger children, starting on the ground is a great idea because it helps them to see the work that you are doing. The bottom-up strategy will take the process of decluttering down to the level of your kid, and helps them stay grounded in the task at hand. Plus, if your child can see where the homes for their items are, this can make it easier for them to develop the habit of placing them there.

## Reinforce the routine that you are setting up with cubbies

You will find that a great tool that you can use is cubbies. These can help kids organize so well, and can kind of give them an experience like they are at school. You can place the cubbies anywhere that they make the most sense in your home, but the entryway of the room can be nice. This becomes a natural drop zone for your child. The cubby allows your child to drop off their stuff, without thinking about it and without making a huge mess everywhere.

## Count to ten

Remember that when your children are helping you out, games are really fun and can help make things easier. When things get messy in the bedroom, make the process of cleaning up feeling like it is a game or play. One game can be to have your child count backward and then get them to pick up ten items to place back in their homes at the end of the day. This can make the chore sound more like a game rather than work, and it can reinforce this good habit in your child at a young age.

## Make sure that you lead by example

This is something that you should do no matter which room of the home you are cleaning. If you want your kids to keep their rooms clean and uncluttered, then you need to do the same thing. Kids are going to mirror what their parents do. If you take the time to go through and declutter the home, this is going to reflect in the work that the kids do as well. Every moment is a lesson with your kids so make sure you develop good decluttering habits as well so that your children learn what is expected.

Cleaning out the room that your kid sleeps in can be an extra challenge. This is their personal space, a place where they not only sleep and dream, but where they hold onto some of their own personal belongings. You need to go through and take some extra steps to make sure that this room is as clean and clutter free as possible.

# Chapter 12: Working on the Office for a More Effective You

The next room that you can take a look at is the home office. This is a special room in the home because each person is going to use it a bit differently. Some will use it to conduct their actual business, and others may use it as a place to relax, a place to keep track of bills, or even a place to store books and other materials. With so many different uses of the home office, it can take some time to actually go through and declutter this room. This chapter is going to spend some time talking about the home office, and providing you with the steps you need to make this room as orderly as possible.

## Identify How You Plan to Use the Office and What is the Most Important

Working from home or having a home office can be a great way to help you stay organized and get things done. But each person is going to use that office in a slightly different manner. But it is hard to do any decluttering in a space when you have no idea how you are going to use that space. If you don't know how you will use the space, then how would you know which items shouldn't and should be found there.

Before you go through the process of decluttering, it is important for you to have a clear picture of what activities already take place, or will take place in that home office. To start, grab a pen and some paper and write down all the ways that you currently use that space. The results of this exercise may provide some good insights to you and can make the decluttering process a bit easier. Some ideas to consider regarding your home office are whether it is a place to:

- Use your printer and computer
- Store journals, magazines, or books
- Store work materials, office supplies, and physical files
- Prepare or collate materials
- Administrative items or process paperwork
- Have webinars, virtual meetings, and telephone calls
- Brainstorm some new ideas
- Review materials
- Think quietly without a bunch of interruptions
- Meet with clients

You can see from this list that there are a ton of things that you can do in your home office, and each of them will allow different items to be found there. Take some time to decide what activities you already do in the office or which ones you plan to do in the future before you go through the process of decluttering that room.

# Remove Anything that is a Household or Personal Item

When you look at your desk, one of the first things that you may notice is that there are a ton of household and personal items around. These may be on, or around your desk, or in other places around the room. There are many reasons why these items end up in your office, but since they aren't related to the work that you are doing, they need to be removed.

Start this process by rounding up all of these household and personal items. These may include things like exercise gear, equipment, books, kitchenware, small appliances, toys, accessories, shoes, and clothing. Depending on how the rest of your office looks, you may need to look around and do a bit of cleaning in order to find some of these unnecessary items. Don't just look at the floor and on the desk to find them. You may need to look under equipment racks and the desk, in storage chests and closets, and even in your filing cabinets and desk drawers to find these items.

Once you have had some time to gather these items, you need to take them and return them back where they really belong in the home. For instance, if you are putting clothing away, put it back in the closet or dresser where it belongs. The toys can go back in your child's room, and the kitchen items can head on back to the kitchen.

## Declutter the Workstation

While it is fine to use office supplies and keep a few personal items at the workstation, you want to make sure that these items aren't so plentiful that you are drowning in them when you should be getting things done. The workspace is your location to get work done, and it should never become a magnet for all that clutter.

To start, take a good look at your workstation. If you need to, get up out of the chair and walk away a bit. This helps you take in the full picture of your workstation and what needs to happen. Consider what the workstation looks like. What is near, beside, behind and on top of your desk, and your chair? Which of those items and which materials and supplies do you use on a daily basis? Which items can you store in another place in your office and which ones can be thrown out?

The first thing to do is throw away anything that is extra on the desk. You can bring in a trash bag to help make this easier. Make it a goal to get rid of at least ten items on the desk that don't belong there. You probably don't need to keep the newspaper from earlier that week or all those extra magazines. There are probably some notes on the desk from past appointments or projects that you don't really need at all either. Throw away all the clutter.

Once that is done, you can move on to sorting through the things that you need to keep. Getting some color-coded folders and other organizational tools can help with this. This helps you to put away the remaining papers and notes and still ensures that the stuff that goes together, such as notes and papers on a specific project, stay together. You can choose the organizational method that you want to go with, just make sure that it removes the clutter and keeps everything as organized as possible.

## Make a Checklist for Decluttering

If you want to make sure that your office is running the best it can and that you won't run into a lot of distractions, then you want to make sure that you keep up with a series of decluttering tasks that you can do on a regular basis. You can include these into your regular work routine to make things easier. Keeping track of the tasks that you want to get done can be as simple as creating a checklist. Aim to take care of these items on a monthly or a weekly, and sometimes even on a daily basis, to ensure that the materials and the mess don't have time to build up on you.

If your office seems to be a magnet for clutter, then take some time each week to do a decluttering session. You can add this into your schedule just like with any other important appointments that you need to take care of. Consider doing it at the end of the week so you have time to get it done, and can have a clean and clear workspace when you come back the following week.

There are a lot of tasks that you can add to your checklist to help you keep your office space looking neat and tidy. The tasks that you choose to do to clean up the home office will vary based on the way that you choose to use that room. Some may choose to use it as an extra room in the home to store important things, and others may find that it works best for them to conduct their business, whether it is a traditional or stay at home job. Some of the items that you may wish to include are:

- Remove any of the personal items that have made it into the office and shouldn't be there.

- Declutter underneath, on the side, and on the top of your desk, or any other area you are working on.

- Pull out old or expired papers and digital files, and get rid of any that you don't need.

- Toss out any assignment materials, programs, and projects that are old.

- Shred the materials and paperwork that need to remain confidential.

- Clean out folders and files from the desktop screen of your computer.

- Declutter your email accounts and folders.

Decluttering out your office is so important for helping you to get more work done, and ensuring that things aren't given time to add up. A clean and clear workspace can make all the difference when it comes to how well you can get the work done. Spend less time trying to find the things that you need, and more time actually getting work done when you implement some decluttering into your week.

# Chapter 13: Cleaning Out the Garage and the Basement

The next two rooms that we are going to talk about are the basement and the garage. These two areas need to have some special attention because they can often be a big mess of clutter. Many people choose to just throw random items in these rooms, items that they want to get out of the way and hope to deal with later, but then they never do.

Because of all this clutter and a lot of time being abandoned, these areas may take some extra time. But with a little bit of planning and taking things in zones, you will be able to clear them out and give yourself a lot of extra space to do what you enjoy. This chapter is going to take some time to show you the basics of cleaning out your garage and your basement so you can finally reclaim those areas for your own needs.

# Decluttering the Garage

First, we are going to take some time to talk about the steps that you can take to declutter your garage. The garage is one area that can attract a lot of mess if you are not careful. Many times, it gets so full of things and so cluttered, that it could be difficult to even get the car through the door. Add in that you often hold a lot of tools, bikes, gardening and yard supplies, and more in there, and it is no wonder that this area will quickly become a mess.

There are a few things that you can do to help clear out the garage. This will give you a lot more space and ensures that you are actually able to get the car into the garage each day. Some of the best tips that you can follow to help declutter your garage include:

- **Take all the items out**: At least get all of the items that you can safely remove out of the garage. This helps you to get a good idea of what was in the garage to start and you can move on from there. Clear out everything, or at least as much as possible.

- **Sort through your finds and work to put similar things together**: This is a really important step when you are trying to make sure that there is some extra space in the garage. For example, put all the hardware together, all the gardening tools, the sporting equipment, and the tools. Do not start putting them back in the garage yet, just leave them in groups so you get a better idea of what you all own.

- **Purse:** After you get everything grouped together, you should have a good idea of what items you own and how many. You may be surprised to see that you have six hammers, and all of them are similar. If this is true in your garage, you should get rid of them. If you have a lot of duplicates of items, or there are lots of damaged items, then get rid of them. This alone may help you to drastically cut down on how many items are in your garage.

- **Organize**: After you have gone through each item that is in your garage, then decide on the things that you want to keep. Now it is time to make a plan of how you would like to store these items so they are easy to get, and will maximize the amount of space that you have. You may want to get a tool cabinet, a pegboard, or even storage bins, and some garages need shelving to help. Try to create a nice storage space in the garage that is off the ground, and can hold some of the items that you have. As you start to put things back away, make sure to label everything so that it is easy to find the items when you need them later on.

- **Rent out some more storage space**: It is preferable if you are able to clean out enough of the clutter in your garage that you can easily fit everything back in there. But in some cases, the garage may be too small or there is some other reason that you just can't fit everything back in there. If this sounds like your garage, then it may be time to rent out some extra storage space. This can help to clear up some extra space around the home and around your garage as well.

Working on your garage can take a bit of time. There are often a lot of items that find their way to the garage, including items for doing the yard work and even boxes of unused items from the home. Make sure that you can spend a few hours in this area so that you can give it the time that it deserves. It is fine for you to split it up into zones as well, to ensure that you are able to get little parts done in the time frame that you have available.

Cleaning out the garage can be an eye-opener. Many times when we follow the steps above, we are going to find that we own a lot of extra items that we never knew we had. Often just combining same items together is enough to empty out a lot of the garage, and if you throw out any item that is damaged or not working well, or that you want to update at a later time, the garage will quickly empty itself out without you missing out on much!

## Decluttering the Basement

The basement can be a difficult area to work with. It often catches a lot of the items that we just box up and put away to get out of sight. But on occasion, it is still a good idea to clear it out to make more room, and to get rid of the things that are just sitting in the way. Some of the steps that you can follow to help you get rid of the clutter in your basement include:

1. **Divide up the basement into zones**: It is important to just work on one part of the basement at a time, especially if the area is large. You can work in one room, on a set of shelves, on the seasonal decorations, on old toys and clothes, or some other part. But just do one thing at a time so you don't become overwhelmed in the process.

2. **Take everything out of the zone**: Let's say that you decided to start with the shelves first. Then the first thing you need to do is take everything off the shelves. If you are working on bins or boxes, then empty the bins out. You should never move on to a second or third zone until you are done with that current zone.

3. **Sort out everything in the basement into two bins**: Since you are in an area that is reserved for storing things, you can remove one of your bins and then focus on

either getting rid of or keeping the items that you find there. If you find things that you want to fix, then create a third bin for items that you can affordably fix. Make sure these have a deadline though, so you don't end up holding onto them for years to come. If you are uncertain about whether you will actually ever fix that item or not, then it is best to just throw it away.

4. **Move the items that you don't plan to keep outside the home**: Before you even think about putting away the items that you would like to keep, take the ones that you choose to get rid of and move them out of the home. Put them right into the trash if you plan to throw them away, or take them to the donation center. This ensures that you get them out of the way and that you don't just shove them right back into the same place again.

5. **Keep things that are similar together**: This is a tip that applies to any room in the home that you are trying to declutter. When you store similar things together, it makes it easier for you to find and access them anytime that you need them down the road. So, put all the Christmas decorations together, all the seasonal clothes together, and so on, to make it easier to find them.

6. **Label the bins and the boxes**: After you have taken the time to sort through the basement, make sure to label everything as you put it back. The better you can label, the easier it will be to find these items later on if you need them. Any type of label will do, just make sure that you are able to see it, that it fully describes what is in that bin or box, and that it won't get ruined down the road.

Cleaning out your basement can take some time. There is often a lot of junk and miscellaneous stuff down there, stuff that you just put down there to get it out of your way. It is fine to spend a few days in this area because it is often a big undertaking, but if you work through each zone one at a time, you are going to see the results. Also, consider the different areas or zones that you would like to set up when you get started with this process. For example, if you have a lot of decorations for the different holidays, consider which zone will work the best for this, so that you can place all of those items next to each other to find them easier later on.

This area can also be difficult because of the number of sentimental things that may be stored down there. Before putting that heirloom back in the box, consider whether you would actually use that in the future and if you actually like the item. If you are just keeping it around because of obligation, then it is time to dump it out. Clearly label everything when you put it back and make sure that it is put away in an orderly fashion, and you will find that it is easier than ever to have a clean basement where everything is easy to find.

# Chapter 14: How to Make That Closet Look Organized

After you have taken some time to clean out all the other rooms in your home, it is time to take a look at the closet. The closet is often the room where you just throw random things that are in the way. And maybe you threw a few items in here as you were decluttering some of the other rooms. Even if you were good about not throwing items into the closet as you cleaned, it is likely that there is still some clutter in these areas from before, and it can be a big eyesore any time you open the door.

But now it is time to open up those closet doors and see what you can do about that mess. Yes, even your closet can be decluttered if you know the right steps to take, and it doesn't have to be as scary as you may think. Let's take a look at some of the tricks that you can employ when it is time to work on decluttering your closet to make the process a bit easier.

## Take just one hour

When you take a look at your closet, you may be overwhelmed by all that needs to get done. There are clothes all over the floor, there are shoes that are everywhere, and you see that purses, blankets, and other things are just hanging around as well. This can make you feel like the work will never be done. One of the best things to do here is to just schedule an hour at a time to help make a dent in that messy closet.

To make this work, bring out a timer and set it for 60 minutes. Or if you can't spare that much time in your busy schedule, split it up into two 30 minute increments through the week. During that time, you just get as much done as possible. Bring in some trash bags to throw broken and old stuff in, as well as some boxes to hold any items that you plan to donate.

This time period is just devoted to working on the closet and getting the following steps done. You should not have any other plans going on at the same time, and if the kids are going to interrupt you often, then it may be best to set up a play date or have someone watch them so you can get your work done. When the timer is done, it is time to stop where you are, put things away, and come back to the work later on.

**Take everything out of the closet**

This may seem like a task, but it can really help you get started. You want to take every last thing that is in the closet out. If you don't take the time to do this, then chances are that the same unworn clothes are just going to be moved around in the closet, rather than being taken care of.

Once you get all the items out of your closet, it is time to sort through it all. Throw out any shoes that are damaged, purses that have missing straps or that are torn, and clothing that is damaged and old. Don't assume that you will fix it up to use later, because you probably won't put in the time to actually do that. Just throw it all out. Then go through and decide what you don't need or wear and donate it. Put everything else back into the closet in an organized manner.

## Take one out each time you put a new one in

Each time that you go to the store and purchase a new item, you need to take an item out of the closet. If you continue to add more things to your closet without ever cleaning it out, you are quickly going to end up with a big mess in there again. You can take an item out and throw it away or donate it, but never add in a new item without clearing out an old one first. This helps you to keep your closet clean.

## Assess the obstacles that are the biggest

Take a look inside your closet and determine what is going to be the biggest obstacle for you to handle. Do you see that you have a ton of shoes that are taking over everything? Go through them and decide which ones you want to keep, and which ones you can get rid of. Then get a hanging shoe rack or an over-the-door organizer to put them in. Do you see that the clothes in your closet are overcrowding everything else? Get some thinner hangers (after clearing out the clothes you will never wear).

Another option you have is to organize the clothes in your closet based on what they are. For example, you can divide up the closet based on jeans, dresses, shirts, and so on, making it easier to find the things that you need. This can bring about some order in your closet, while also saving you some time when looking for an outfit in the morning.

## Treat your wardrobe like it is a time capsule

Many times we hold onto clothes, shoes, and other items that we never use just because they hold a special meaning to us, or because we hope to someday be able to wear them. But that dress that you haven't worn since high school, or those skinny jeans that are still six sizes too small when you haven't eaten healthily or worked out in months is simply taking up room. It is time to go through and get rid of anything that isn't part of your signature look.

This signature look includes all the outfits that you wear on a regular basis. These are the clothes that make you look good, and the ones that make you feel comfortable, so you are more likely to wear them. Sure, that dress may look nice, and that suit outfit may seem really cool in the closet, but if they are just sitting there and never being used, then they are not worth your time.

Essentially, when you combine together all your articles of clothing, including shirts, dress clothes, pants, sweaters, and shoes, you should only have about 30 to 40 pieces. This is plenty to mix and match to get all the different styles and looks that you want. Anything that doesn't make the list should be donated or tossed out to clear up space in your closet.

## Ask some questions that may be tough

When you are looking through the closet, you need to think through a lot of hard questions about each item you take out. Besides asking when was the last time that you wore a particular article of clothing, you should also ask some other questions including:

- Is this article a representation of my fantasy self or my self that I wish I could be? Or is it something that I would actually wear?

- Do I need to weigh a certain amount in order to feel good while wearing this article of clothing?

- Is the upkeep a pain for this article of clothing? Is it

only dry clean, does it show wear and tear easily, or do you need to iron it before you can wear it again? Is the upkeep really worth your time?

- The last time that I put this article on, how did I feel?

If your answer on these questions is negative, then you may want to get rid of that item. If it is something that is bulky but you treasure it because it's an heirloom, or has a lot of sentimental value, then you can consider putting those items in storage somewhere to get them out of the way.

## Don't consider the return on investment

Many people will hold onto an item because it cost them an arm and a leg and they want to get their money's worth out of that item. But instead of actually using that item, they will just stuff it back into the closet for another time, and encounter the same problem the next time they try to declutter. If you are looking for the return on investment with all the items in your closet, you are going to be holding onto a lot of items that you shouldn't.

Sure, you may have spent a lot of money on that designer name bag or on those shoes, but if you never actually use those items, then it is just collecting dust and taking up space. Instead, learn from that mistake and don't make it again in the future, and then donate that item or give it away to someone who may actually get some use out of it.

Cleaning out the closet can be a big chore. A lot of things have gotten shoved in there throughout the time, and when you finally decide to go through it, the place can be a horrible mess. Figuring out what you should get rid of and what you should keep can be a hassle. But following the steps above can really help make it easier to complete.

# Chapter 15: Daily Tips to Make Decluttering Your Life Easier

Decluttering your life doesn't have to be difficult, even though it may take some time depending on how messy your home is. The hardest part is coming up with a plan and getting started so that you can start seeing the results. Some of the tips that you can follow when it is time to start decluttering your home includes:

**Engage others to help out around the house**

Decluttering the home and keeping it looking nice does not have to be just your job. Many times, only one person is doing all the work, and this can get exhausting. If you are constantly picking up and decluttering everything in the home, you can feel resentful and may be more likely to give up because nothing ever seems to get done. A better approach is to get everyone in your home involved in the process.

There are a ton of benefits to doing things this way. First, it takes some of the work off your shoulders. Instead of you having to go through every room in the house and declutter and instead of only you having to make sure the house stays decluttered, you can get everyone on board with the idea to help.

This can include your husband, your kids if they are old enough, and everyone else. When you share the work, it doesn't seem as bad to handle and you won't feel you are fighting an uphill battle. Lastly, everyone in the home will start to appreciate the effort that it takes, and how nice the home feels when the decluttering process is done.

## Do the dishes once you are done cooking or after a meal

No one likes to do the dishes. There is just something about them that can make everyone annoyed, and many quickly run to find something else to get done instead. And it doesn't help that those dishes need to be taken care of a few times a day, or they seem to pile up. Many of us put off doing dishes until the end of the night, or even wait a few days before touching the dishes, simply because we don't like to do them. Then, by the time we get to them, they have lots of stuck on food particles, the piles are high, and the work has multiplied.

One thing that you can do to help keep your kitchen looking nice and organized, is to just do the dishes when a meal is done. This will only include a few dishes at a time, unless you really had a messy prep for the meal, and can ensure that the kitchen always looks nice and clean. It may seem like a big hassle, but having all the dishes put away and looking nice can go a long way in helping declutter that kitchen of yours.

In addition to taking some time to clean the dishes after you are done with the meal, spend a few minutes tidying up the rest of the kitchen, and even the rest of the home. If you have done well with maintaining the decluttering since you did the main process, and you have gotten everyone else on board to help you out, you can spend ten to fifteen minutes each night maintaining the cleanliness, before you can sit down and relax for the night with a clean home.

If you have some time, and a little bit of ambition, take this time to prepare yourself for the next day. For example, you can easily set out your keys, the clothes you want to wear the next day, the homework for your kids, and anything else that you need to take to work with you the following day. Most people don't need a ton of items to help them get started for the next day, but it is always easier to do it right away at night, rather than scrambling around in the morning when you are tired.

## Listen to some music when you clean up

Nothing motivates quite as well as some good music. If you have a lot of decluttering to get done, or you need to get a lot of cleaning done in a short amount of time, then turn on the radio or your own music player and get to work right away.

Studies have shown how positive and upbeat music can make all the difference when it comes to how much work you can get done. It can help you to focus on the task at hand, it can set the speed at which you clean, and it can even help you to be in a better mood while decluttering. You can be the one who chooses the type of music, but something that helps you be upbeat and stay focused on the task at hand can make a big difference.

## Set a timer to get the tasks done

Many of us like to procrastinate when it comes to getting tasks done. We think it is going to take forever to finish, and we just don't want to put in the time to make it happen. Instead of getting started with the work and just getting it done, we keep putting it off, only doing a little bit at a time, and other tasks that make it very hard to ever get anything done. We end up with a self-fulfilling prophecy of the task actually taking as long as we feared.

If we just got on top of that task right away, rather than messing around, things wouldn't be so bad. And this is where the timer can come in to help. When you are ready to do a task, set your timer and then get to work. Set it for fifteen to twenty minutes (most tasks won't take longer than this if you really get to work), and then spend that time just focusing on that task. You may even be able to get the task done faster, then move on to another one and see what you can get done in that time.

Often our fear of getting started on a new task is because we are worried that it will take too long.

But most of the tasks that we need to complete don't take as long as you think they will. Just set that timer and don't focus on anything else until it is done.

**Don't rely on storage units**

One trap that a lot of people will fall into when they are decluttering their lives, is the idea that they can just move their items to storage units. They will go through a lot of the topics that we discussed in this guidebook, and then add in another pile; a pile that allows them to move their unused items to a storage unit. All this does is move the clutter to another area, rather than letting you deal with it.

If you choose to rely on a storage unit, you are just making the process worse. It is easy to grab some items and move it to the storage unit, knowing that it is still there if you need it. You aren't learning how to get rid of items that you don't need for good, then you will continue to purchase more items, and keep going through the same process that got you in this mess to start with.

In addition to still keeping around the clutter, even though it is moved to a new location, you are adding another bill to your month. Now, you not only pay the mortgage on your home, but you are also spending money to maintain an area that just holds onto your junk and clutter. This is a horrible way to waste money just to make decluttering easier when it actually makes the process more difficult.

If you want to take an item and place it in storage, then that is probably a good sign that you should just get rid of the item. Most of the time, when you put something in the storage unit, you will completely forget about it. They will keep paying the storage unit fee each month, and then never see those items for two, three, or more years. This is just a waste of your time and money. It is much better for you to take that item and donate it, or throw it away. You aren't going to use that item anyway, so you may as well throw it out rather than spending money on a storage unit that holds your trash.

## Plan out what you need to do tomorrow

Each night before you head to bed, take some time to make plans for the next day. When we wake up in the morning, we are often tired and worn out. We are trying to get up and get some things done. We are trying to get out the door for work, and school, and everything else. It is hard to get our minds to work and remember all the things that need to be done.

This is why you should make a plan the night before and write it down. Find everything important that you need right away in the morning, get the coffee pot ready to go, and lay out the clothes for the kids. Write down everything that you need to get done in the morning before you even head off to work. If there is something important that you need to get done at some other time of the day, write that information down as well.

This process only has to take about five minutes at night, but it can really help make your day better. It keeps you more organized, helps you to stay on track, and prevents some of the big issues that can come up when you spend most of your morning searching around for your keys or other items.

# Chapter 16: Different Techniques You Can Use to Make Decluttering a Breeze

The topic of decluttering is a large one, and because of this, many people have come up with their own techniques to make decluttering easier than ever. There are actually many methods that you can use to help declutter your home, your mind, and everything else in your life. Let's take a look at some of the best methods that you can choose when you are worried about getting started with decluttering.

## KonMarie Method

This is a method that was made popular by Marie Kondo, and it is actually one of the most popular and a well-known method for decluttering that is out there. The core idea behind this method is that instead of deciding what you want to get rid of when you clean your home, you will instead choose what you would like to keep, and then declutter the rest.

To start out with this method, you will collect every item that you own that fits in a particular category and then add it to one large pile. For example, you may be working on clothes at this time so you would go and collect every t-shirt that you own and lay them out on the bed. Then take each one and hold it, feel it, or wear it to help you get a sense of how it makes you feel.

While you are wearing that item, ask if it brings a spark of joy to your heart or not? Depending on how you feel about that item, you will decide whether or not to keep that item and then move on to the next. You can do this with every item that you own if you want.

The positives of the KonMarie method are that it is very thorough, and it allows you to compare all the items that you have that are similar. This helps you to easily get rid of any duplicates that are out there, and you can easily compare items that you don't like as much or that are well-worn, to newer and better item, resulting in an easy way to get rid of some of the old. It is a very effective way to make progress when you are trying to declutter specific categories that have been spread around the house.

However, this method can be very time-consuming and will mean that you need to sort through a whole bunch of stuff in this manner. Instead of focusing on just doing one room or two rooms at a time, you are going through and pulling out things from the whole house, and this could cause quite a mess when you try to clean up.

## The Minimalist Game

This is a method that is going to take the experience that comes with decluttering and turns it into a game. It is a popular method of decluttering where hundreds of people will use their #minsgame hashtag on social media each month.

The basics of this game is that on the first day of the month, the number of things that you are going to declutter will correspond with the day of the month. So, on the first day of the month, you will declutter one item, on the second day, you get rid of two items, and so on. By the time you get to the end of the month, you will remove 496 items from the home if you make it all the way through. This becomes even more fun if you can challenge a friend or a family member to see who can keep going with this for the longest.

One benefit of doing this is that when the month is done, if you keep up with it, you will have gotten rid of a ton of stuff. Removing 300 items from your home is a big task, and you can play for as many months as you would like. It helps that you start out small and then increase the amount over time. This can be nice for those who are looking to build up their confidence in their decision-making abilities, and you will get better at letting stuff go.

There are some negatives that come with this method. A major issue with it is that you need to stay consistent with this or you are going to fall behind. Much like Tetris, the difficult is going to increase each level and it can be difficult to keep up once you fall behind. And when you reach the end of the month, you may find that it is a bit overwhelming to find 20 some items to get rid of when you are tired from work.

## The Four Box Method

Another method that you may want to try out is one that is known as the four box method. This is a flexible method that can help you deal with all the items that are cluttering up your home. You can do it for however long you want and the frequency you prefer. By sorting the clutter into four categories, you are going to make a decision for every item that is out of place in your home.

The basic with this method is that you will go into a room and label four boxes. These can be labeled as put away, give away, undecided, and throw away. Then you will go through the room and pick up the clutter that is there and place it in one of those four boxes. Every item needs to go into one of those boxes. The undecided box is a nice addition because you can put stuff in there that you are not sure about, but if you want to have a plan for everything, then get rid of this one box.

The positive of working with this method of decluttering is that it is pretty easy to understand, and there is a category available for everything. The items that go in the undecided box are ones that you will reconsider later at some other time. This gives you a lot of flexibility and lets you declutter the room at the pace that works the best for you.

The issue with this method is that if you are not careful, that undecided box can become a big problem as more things start to pile up inside it. If you are worried about misusing this box, consider going down to three boxes so you will actually make a decision about all the items.

## One Method

If you like the ideas that come with a few of these methods, then the one method is the best for you. This method was created by taking similar philosophies and combining them together into one concept that is easy to understand. The idea behind this one is that you will get rid of just one thing every day for a set period of time. You can pick out how long you want to do this for. Many start with a month and then move from there. The one thing that you get rid of can be one item, one box that is filled, one filled up bag, or anything else that works the best for you.

The benefit of the One Method is that it can help you to build up a habit of decluttering without taking too much effort.

Since you just have to get rid of one thing every day, you are learning how to build decluttering into your daily routine, so all that clutter doesn't end up coming back and being in the way. Another benefit that comes with this method is that you can create your own system, and you can choose how much you want to get rid of (single item versus a box full) depending on your activity level, and how much you need to get all cleaned up.

Due to the consistency that is required for this method and for some people with a busy schedule, it can be hard to keep up with. Or if there are times when you need to be away from home, this is going to be difficult to keep up as well. This method wouldn't work well for those who want to do the work in a big burst, rather than little steps either.

## Packing Party

Another method that you can try out is a fairly common method, and it is one that you are already using if you plan to move into a new location. While it does take some preparation to make it work, and you may need to enlist some help from friends, it can be effective if you can make it through.

The basics of this one is you will have some people come over, and pack everything that you own into boxes as if you are about to move. Then, through the next few months or so, only take out the items that you actually use. After three months have passed, any item that is left in the box needs to be donated or sold because you aren't likely to use it.

One of the benefits of this method is that it can definitely help you get rid of the items that you don't use. Things that are out of sight can often be out of mind, and you may not miss a lot of the items that are in the box. It can take some time to accomplish, but it ensures that you are getting rid of everything that you no longer needs.

The negative of this method is that it may not make a ton of sense unless you are already in the process of packing up to move. Not only does it take up a ton of energy and time, you already have to go out searching for, or purchasing boxes to make this happen. And it may not work well if you have some seasonal items or items that you only take out a few times a year anyway.

## The Closet Hanger Method

The final method that we are going to talk about is one that helps you figure out what items in the home you actually use. This method allows you to track exactly what has been used in your home, without having to go through such massive methods like the packing party.

As the name suggests, you are going to work on cleaning out your closet, but you can adjust it to some other items as well. When you begin, turn all the hangers in the closet to face the same direction. As you war the items, you will put them back into the closet, but you will turn the hanger around the opposite direction to help show that you actually wore that item. Over time, you will be able to tell which items you actually wear, and which ones are just sitting in the closet and taking up space.

This type of decluttering method is really easy to implement and doesn't take you a ton of time to get started with. It is a clear-cut way to see just what you are using out of your closet and what you don't use. This method works the best for helping you to clean out your closet, and get rid of the clothes that you no longer wear, but you can certainly adjust it to help you declutter other items throughout your home.

Since this method is specifically designed to help with clothing, it can be difficult depending on what other items you want to get rid of. Plus, if you have any items that need to be folded and put in your dresser, this method won't work as well. You need to have some discipline to make sure that the clothing item gets put back into your closet, and facing the right way after you wear it, or this method is not going to work.

For items that aren't considered clothing and can't be hung up, this method can be hard to work with and you may not be sure what method to use, or what variation to use, to make it work. This is another method that doesn't work well with items that are for special occasions, or for any of the seasonal items that you own.

These are some of the most popular decluttering methods that you can choose to implement into your cleaning process. All of these can be implemented to give you some great results with how clean your home can be, and can be used with the different strategies that we talked about before. Take a look at some of these methods, and decide which one will work the best for your particular cleaning style and for decluttering your home.

# Conclusion

Decluttering your home, as well as other parts of your life can really make a difference. You are going to feel less stressed out. You can spend less time worrying about cleaning the house, and more time doing the things that you love. You can actually take up a hobby, spend time with friends and family, and just enjoy life.

Our modern society has put too much emphasis on owning material possessions. We think that we will be able to find happiness with material things. And the advertisements that we see around us all the time do nothing to help with this issue. Many people have started to assign feelings and value to items that shouldn't be there, and this makes it very easy to collect more, and hard to let these things go.

Decluttering and minimalism work against this idea. While you don't have to get rid of everything in your home to follow these ideas, it is important to realize what can stay and what needs to go. Holding onto things just because you think they are valuable, or because you give them extra value in your head that shouldn't be there, and we refuse to let items go when they are just in the way. With decluttering, it is time to let go of these things, and learn which items to keep that actually bring us some happiness.

This guidebook took some time to talk about decluttering and why it is such an important process to work on. We took a look at some of the basics that come with decluttering, what the minimalist lifestyle is like and why it can be so beneficial, some of the top reasons that people refuse to get started with decluttering their own lives, and so much more.

We then moved on to some of the steps that you can take to declutter every room in your home. Remember, you only need to work on one room at a time and only for an hour or so at a time. If you get overwhelmed, or you have a busy schedule and need to take a bit longer, then that is fine. This is the beauty of working with decluttering, as long as you make progress forward, and don't start reintroducing more stuff back into the home at the same time, then you are doing it the right way.

This guidebook ends with some tips to make the decluttering process easier, along with a discussion about which methods are popular, and how you can get each one to work. All of the methods can work, you just need to pick out the one that you can stick with, the one that will work the best for you and your style of cleaning out the clutter.

When you are ready to make some changes in your life, and finally get rid of all the stuff that is in your home, all the stuff that you constantly need to clean up and that is always in the way, all the stuff that takes up your time away from the people and things you really love, then this guidebook is for you. It will show you all the steps you need to take to finally get rid of that clutter for good.

# Book 2:
# Declutter Your Mind

Life Changing Ways to Eliminate Mental Clutter, Relieve Anxiety, and Get Rid of Negative Thoughts Using Simple Decluttering Strategies for Clarity, Focus, and Peace

# Introduction

As a parent or a busy career-minded person, you may find that your life feels like a whirlwind of go, go, go. There are times that your mind will be so cluttered with all the details of what you need to do for the day, that you find it hard to shut down at night. This can lead to countless hours tossing and turning at night with no real sleep. That is when insomnia sets in and you start to walk around cranky and in a daze—due to lack of sleep and motivation. If this sounds all too familiar to you, then I know exactly how you feel.

I used to spend countless hours out of the night tossing and turning, worried about all the things that I needed to do the next day. I would spend my time throughout the day rushing to get all my to-dos done—only to find that there were more to-dos than I realized. I would be overwhelmed, stressed out, and snippy with my loved ones. I found myself saying, "Do not add more stuff to my plate." I would beg my kids to just sit down and be quiet. I found that no matter how much stuff I got done within the day, it was never enough. I always had more to do, and I felt like my list would never end. I was burning the wick at both ends.

I was burned out and stressed out, and I could feel my mental health declining. I noticed that how I felt was starting to be an everyday occurrence and that it was simply not how I wanted to live. I knew that my family deserved more and that I deserved to be happy and not so stressed out. That is when I started to work on my stress levels and my to-do lists. I decided that I needed to declutter my whole life. I started with my household environment and moved on to my mindset and mental health. I built a routine that worked better for me, with healthier choices and exercise added in. I noticed that once I started to gain a better handle on the clutter within my mind, my to-do list started to decrease, and I was able to accomplish more in my day with larger amounts of time for self-care and family commitments.

I knew that others were suffering just as I had, and I knew that living a cluttered life was creating more health problems for me and creating relationship difficulties for my friends and family. I worked so hard to improve my life and make things much less cluttered and stressful. With all the knowledge that I learned while decluttering my life, I knew that I had to share this information with the world. That is when I sat down and decided to write this manual to help you accomplish the same decluttering within your mind that I have been able to do for myself. I had written about my process, and I knew that it would make a good piece of groundwork for this book.

Decluttering Your Mind is a well-thought-out resource manual that is designed to teach you how clutter and stress can affect your life and show you how to declutter your mind and build a new routine that will help you accomplish much more in life. When your mind is cluttered with social media overwhelm, tasks that need to be accomplished, negative thoughts, and relationships that are not healthy—you will be more stagnant than you wish to be. The clutter will block you from getting things accomplished, and you will find that your relationships begin to suffer along with your life goals. You will experience large amounts of overwhelm and find that you are spending more time in a constant state of stress and chaos than happiness.

Happiness is not a luxury. It is something that we all are capable of feeling. Many people do not feel happiness in their lives simply because they allow the wrong people and the wrong thoughts to invade their happy space. This is due in part to the clutter that is blocking them from thinking positively about life as well as blocking them from moving forward with their life goals.

With this book, you will learn how to develop a new daily routine that will improve your ability to organize your goals and create a more well-rounded lifestyle. This will allow you to be less stressed on a daily basis and give you positive insight into how you can adjust your mindset and start to create a less cluttered mind with more room to advance and grow. Everyone lives with stress and clutter, but you do not have to. By following the processes and details within this book, you will be able to gain more insight and change how you are living your life. You will be able to feel less chaos in your life—and with that, you should be able to improve your mental health and your sleep patterns.

Decluttering Your Mind is a book designed with you in mind. None of the activities or recommendations will be too difficult, and each one can be done whether you are a parent or a career-minded adult. With each chapter, you will gain more insight and helpful tips or tools to increase your mental health status; declutter your mind and the thoughts that are blocking you from improving your life; as well as create better relationships with friends, family, and co-workers.

The first few chapters will be about how clutter in your mind affects everything in your life and creates stress. The rest of the chapters will teach techniques that you can use to de-stress, declutter, and build a new daily habit that will improve your mental capacity and help you continue living a happy life.

# Chapter 1: Why People Live With Cluttered Minds

For years, people have wondered if the way someone keeps their desk or home is how they feel inside — and I hate to tell you that it absolutely, unequivocally means that they feel cluttered inside.

Those who are living in a space that is cluttered and chaotic oftentimes feel the same way in their mind and in their heart. Studies have shown that those who are born with that non-linear style of thinking will be hardwired to think more artistically and less organized. They tend to think of starting a project instead of filing the taxes. These are the type of people that would come home and jump on the next great project before they finish the first five that they started prior to this one. They will be the ones that you walk in and find them with papers on all of the counters with no clear organization or strategy.

Those non-linear thinkers will clear their internal space by only spending time focused on how to have the most creative time for projects instead of maintaining an organized and strategic desk or home environment.

Another aspect of why people live with clutter inside their minds and their homes is simply due to the connection that they feel towards the items that they need to dispose of. Many people have emotional connections to the clutter and these connections have created physical pain in then they are forced to remove those thoughts or items from their minds or households.

Even perfectionist will deal with the clutter within the mind or home. They do so to deal with the compulsion to be ready whenever they need to be for whatever they need to be ready for. Many people also feel a need to hold on to thoughts, experiences, friends, and even items that will bring them some sort of emotion that they can connect with on a different level.

Many people tend to hold on to these things that are cluttering up their life because they know what to expect from these things. They are predictable, and this makes them more comfortable with these unpleasant emotions, or items within their mind or home. For instance, what are you accustomed to dealing with in your mind? What mental clutter have you been managing without simply letting it go?

Being overwhelmed with social media accounts is another way that people are allowing clutter to interfere in their lives. Below I will go into more detail about social media and clutter, but for now, let us talk about how many apps do you visit in one day?

If you are anything like me, you may log in to Facebook several times per day. If Facebook is not your thing, so instead you log into Instagram several times per day. Have you ever sat down and actually looked into how many hours a day you spend on social media?

Just for fun, pull out a notebook and sit down with at least 30 minutes to sketch out a detailed schedule of how much time you have spent on social media that day. It is best if you start this task on a Monday and make a record of each day for one week.

Once you get a good basis for the amount of time that you spend on social media you will be able to see how much overwhelm you are experiencing from social media and the use of social media. When I did this activity, I realized that I was spending large quantities of time, that I could be using in other useful ways, on social media. This was eating into my time that I normally would have spent on schoolwork or on improving myself. This was quite an astonishing thing to see. I knew that I spent a large quantity of time on social media on Facebook, Instagram, Pinterest, and Twitter. I realized that these were overwhelming my mental clutter and placing me in a constant state of chaos.

I realized that I needed to change my habits and later in this book I will go over some ways that you make changes to your social media habits to help better serve you and eliminate the mind clutter and overwhelm that you feel from using so much social media.

The point I am getting at is that no matter what it is that is cluttering up your brain and your life there are ways to fix these things and move to a more productive less cluttered way of living.

In this book, I will walk you through several steps that will help you get to a less cluttered life. If you are ready to make real changes, then while you are reading this book, I suggest you sit down with a notebook so that you can do the activities and take notes about your life and how you will begin to declutter it.

This book is designed to help you with simple tasks and activities that will increase your ability to handle stress, declutter your mind, relationships and home, as well as add healthier habits to your day. The systematic process that is detailed in this book is designed to help you incorporate several positive activities into your daily routine as well as teach you how to develop those new positive routines with ease.

When you set out to make positive changes in your life there will be lots of resistance, this is only normal. The key to fighting the resistance and building a new more effective lifestyle with less clutter and healthier friendships is to have a plan that is well thought out and strategic. The tools that you will need to do this properly can be found between the chapters within this book. I will be going over several useful tips and methods that have helped me find less clutter in my life as well as improve my health, my sleeping habits, and my ability to set goals and accomplish them effectively. Each chapter holds several activities that can be accomplished by downloading the workbook at the back of this book or by creating one that works better for you. I have included the workbook for the explicit reason of helping you to improve your lifestyle and declutter your life so you can feel more confident, accomplished, healthy, and active in the appropriate ways for growth and stability.

# Chapter 2: What Happens When We Are Overwhelmed With So Much Social Media

Social media is a big piece of everyone's life. If you are not on social media, then you are in your elderly years or you simply do not find social media interesting. If this is the case, then this section of the chapter would not work for you. But if you are on social media like the rest of the world this section will be shocking when you find out how social media is cluttering up your mind.

The amount of time that people spend on social media in one day may not be surprising to you, but many people find that the national average for checking social media once every 12 minutes is quite low. But what they do not realize is that they are checking their phones over 80 times per day. Each time you check your phone you are spending over 10 minutes on one of the many social media sites that are available to use. One study showed that some people get aggravated if they are not able to check their phone every 4 minutes. This means that on average they may check their phone 48 times per day, with each time averaging 10 minutes per check. That means you are spending 480 minutes checking their phone. That gives you a total of 8 hours per day on social media.

When you look at this figure you may be quite shocked. To think you work 8-hours per day at a full-time job and then spend another 8-hours per day checking on social media within a 12-hour period. That is an impressive amount of time to spend on social media.

So, what does this mean for you and your mental clutter? Simply put if you are spending 8-hours per day on social media then you are working a full-time job by checking your social media accounts. This may seem like a huge waste of time to you now, whereas before, you may have thought it was just a normal behavior for someone who used social media on a regular basis.

Now that you have a clear view of how much time you may be spending on social media then you can guess how this is impacting your life. By occupying your time with social media apps, you are distracting yourself from activities that could be pushing you farther in life and advancing your growth and knowledge, or you could be spending time participating in self-care activities.

## How Mental Clutter Can Create Chaos in Your Life
**Brain**

Stress has a tendency to build up cortisol within your brain. This can be a long-term effect which is created by long-term exposure to stress. When you have chronic stress, it can lead to many horrible health issues. Cortisol is part of the processes that the body uses naturally for restore balance, regulate the blood sugar, and helps with the hippocampus. The hippocampus is the location that the memories are stored within your brain. This is also the location that the memories are processed and categorized.

When you experience chronic stress, the body will overproduce the cortisol and it is then released into the bloodstream. This is when your body can go into health-related trouble. Too high of a level of cortisol can actually wear down the brains functioning abilities, and this can create a disruption in the regulation of the synapsis. This will eventually result in a loss of the need to socialize as well as the need to avoid all interactions with other people. Simply put stress kills brain cells and has been known to reduce the brain size of someone that is overstressed. This can explain why those that are overwhelmed and stressed are not able to make proper decisions and tend to make poor choices.

By shrinking the prefrontal cortex, you begin to lose memory and also lose your learning ability. Although the stress levels are able to shrink your cortex it can also increase your amygdala, and this will just perpetuate the receptiveness of stress, which increases the stress levels. Cortisol will create a sort of domino effect that creates a hard-wired pathway which is located between the hippocampus and amygdala which will help to create vicious cycles of the brain becoming predisposed for a constant fight or flight response.

## Psychological

Research has shown that there are physical connections between stress and your mental health. Many people who suffer from stress also suffer from PTSD or post-traumatic stress disorder. The ratio of those with the white matter as well as gray matter is much higher in the people who suffer from a stress-related mental health disorder. Those who are dealing with chronic stress levels will have a much whiter matter in specific areas of the brain.

Gray matter is composed of two specific types of cells which are called neurons. These neurons will process the information and then store it within the glia. Glia is a cell that gives support to the neurons. Since white matter is mostly composed of the axons, that are formed to create fiber networks, they aid in the connection of neurons. The cells that were focused on when studying the effects of the brain and stress were the myelin that is located within the brain.

Hippocampus is used to regulate the emotions and memories within the brain. Science has shown that the neural stem cells act differently when exposed to stress. When under stress the cells will become an oligodendrocyte, which is a myelin-producing cell structure. These types of cells will help with the synapses, which connects the communication tools that are needed for allowing the nerve cells to transfer information.

With chronic stress, you will receive more myelin-producing cells with a bit more neurons. This will disrupt the total balance within the brain which causes a delay in communication of the cells of the brain. Due to this, there are more problems within the brain.

The point that I am trying to make with this is that due to all of those aspects the people who suffer from stress disorders, including those similar to PTSD, will have altered brain connections. This can lead to a connection that is stronger within the hippocampus as well as the prefrontal cortex. If you are having amygdala and hippocampus connections that are stronger, then the response would be more rapid fear setting in. If the connection is much weaker, then the ability to calm the brain and shut off stress is impaired. Those suffering from stressful situations will have an imbalance that limits their response and shut down.

Another key factor that plays a role in how stress will damage our brain is found when you look at the oligodendrocyte cells. Through this research, they found that these cells will become myelin-producing and they affect the functions that are cognitive. Since the neurons are processed and transmitted with the electrical information that is needed for the memory skills and learning that you will be doing.

Although there is not a ton of information on how stress is affecting your psychological well-being it is clearly an issue for your whole body. That is why stress is not something you should wish to keep in your life.

## The Effect of Stress on Your Body

Stress can have many effects on your body. It is not something that simply hides in the background. Stress will affect your attitude, your communication levels, your brain functioning, your physical well-being, your psychological well-being, and the well-being of those around you. Stress has a way of turning your world upside down.

What you can expect from stress is more headaches, insomnia, a decrease in your productivity, as well as disinterest in some of your favorite activities. Stress has a way of taking you out of your comfort zone and making you feel like everything is wrong. You will have higher blood pressure, heart disease, obesity, and even diabetes. Stress has been known to be the contributing factor for the majority of the heart attack victims every year. When you leave stress unchecked, you can end up unhealthier than you were prior to taking on all the stress.

## Common Side Effects of Stress in Your Body:

- Change in sex drive
- Fatigue
- Headache

- Chest pain
- Sleep problems
- Muscle tension or pain
- Stomach upset

**Common Effects of Stress on Your Mood:**

- Lack of motivation
- Anxiety
- Irritability
- Restlessness
- Anger
- Depression
- Overwhelmed Feelings
- Lack of focus
- Sadness

**Common Effects of Stress on Your Behavior**

- Angry outbursts
- Overeating

- Drug or alcohol abuse
- Undereating
- Act to manage stress
- Tobacco use
- Exercising less often
- Social withdrawal

If you are experiencing any of these symptoms, then you will need to take some medical steps to manage the stress that you are feeling. There are many medical and non-medical ways to manage your stress. These can be incorporated into your daily activities to help reduce stress as well as reduce the mental clutter.

## Actionable tips:

- Start a new hobby.
- Start a regular physical activity or exercise routine.
- Listen to your favorite music.
- Spend time with those you love.

- Enjoy a great laugh.
- Practice meditation or mindfulness.
- Taichi
- Go to a massage studio.
- Breathe deep.
- Relax in a bath.
- Read your favorite book.
- Practice yoga.

There are several ways that you can actively reduce your stress. However, there are just as many inactive ways to manage your stress. These inactive ways tend to be more of a stress producer in the long run though. So, try to avoid using these inactive ways to reduce your stress that are listed below.

- watching your favorite television show
- going on the Internet and using social media
- playing your favorite video game

**One of the healthiest ways to reduce your stress is to get a balance between**:

- Diet
- Sleep
- avoid using alcohol
- tobacco
- illicit drugs
- caffeine

Whatever you choose to utilize as a way to de-stress, simply make sure it is healthy and not creating more stress in your life. Often times, people will fill their time with inactive ways to de-stress and although they may feel as if they are accomplishing an effective de-stress method in their lives, they really are creating more struggle and opposition within their bodies. By using inactive methods to de-stress you are causing some simple chemical changes to take place within your mind and body that will eventually create more problems and could change the way you live, ultimately. For instance, if you avoid stress by watching TV and binge eating junk, then you will eventually be heavier and lazier in life. If you are using caffeine to de-stress you will find that you have less energy throughout the day and you will also begin to develop kidney stones and put on mid-section weight gain. By using illicit drugs or alcohol to de-stress you are creating bad habits that could end up with chronic disease and even death.

The goal in life is not to let the stress take control. It is to simply manage the stress that we are faced with everyday with healthy habits that keep us happy, alive, and healthy. Caffeine, alcohol, drugs, fatty foods, social media, TV binge watching, and so many other inactive ways to deal with stress can create more complications and even derail our life goals. They can limit our ability to sleep which adds more stress to our lives and then you will find yourself in a cycle of bad habits that are unhealthy and derailing.

# Chapter 3: Tips to Limit Your Overwhelm and Be More Productive.

By limiting the amount of information, that you have going into your mind, this will eliminate the overload that you feel throughout the day.

## Limiting Your Information Overload

Doing a brain dump can help you get things out of your head. It allows you to be more productive and clear the mind of any clutter and stress that would create chaos in your life. To brain dump, you will be able to empty all the crap that has built up in your mind and all those emotional moments that have been stored within your mind that are still holding you back from completing the goals that you set out to do. By writing things down immediately, especially those that are interrupting your workflow. This process allows you to get those thoughts out of the head and clear your brain for a better way to function without the difficulty of focusing on your favorite activities. This act of decluttering your brain with a brain dump is giving yourself permission to relax and allow things to start to happen organically.

Once you have written down all the information that you have brain dumped out of your head then you can begin to place them in an organized list by priority. This can be set up as things that need to be done today, things that you can pass on to someone else to do, things that will need to be done in a week, and of course things that you can completely eliminate from your to-do list. If you locate something in this process that just does not seem to go away, it may be a task that is not properly defined or something that is not actionable at this time. This can be those things that will take more time to decide on, such as taking a trip or moving to another area. These tasks can then be broken into subcategories that will allow for you to take the steps that are necessary one by one until you have completed the whole goal.

## Avoiding Social Media Early in the Morning

To avoid social media early in the morning is a great way to start your day without jumping down that rabbit hole of Facebook, Instagram, and Pinterest. When working the notifications that you receive from these types of apps can be distracting as well. So, first thing in the morning you should shut down all notifications and avoid using the apps prior to getting ready for your day. When you first wake up you will need to start your day with a mindfulness of meditative practice. This will help you to start your day on the positive note that you need to decrease the mental clutter that has arose when the sun came up. Another action that should be taken first thing in the morning is the act of journaling or reading for 30 minutes per day. This engages your brain and creates a space of self-care and learning which will help clear out the mental clutter that has been blocking your form moving forward in life.

Journaling has been talked about further down in this book, for now, I just want to touch lightly on the way you can incorporate it into your day while eliminating the need to jump straight to social media. We are all excited to find out what happened overnight to our friends, family, and those that we follow on social media, but what we need to realize is that those posts will be there when you are ready to check them out. Since social media is a storehouse of other people's words, thoughts, and messages it is safe to say that when you get to it you will not have missed anything important. So, take some time first thing in the morning to check in with yourself. This will help you feel more confident about greeting the day ahead of you, and then you will be able to start the day on a more positive note which will help with he is decluttering of your mind and the chaos or stress that has arisen.

A few things that you can replace your habit of checking social media first thing in the morning can be found below:

**Use a two-minute rule for completing sub-tasks.**

If you are dealing with needing lots of little tasks that are necessary to complete, then you should designate 45 minutes to 2 hours out of your day to work on tasks that will plow through those items that will take no more than 2 minutes to complete. This can be tasks such as email, tidying your home, checking in with financial records or accounts, or phone calls and such.

**Block similar tasks together so that they can be completed quickly.**

If you are working on tasks that are similar in nature it is best to block them together and complete them all at once. If you are needing to clean your home do not do simply organize the closet, instead of the whole house. When you complete a task that is similar to another you can stay focused on each one of them until they are completed by completing the first one and then the next one in an organized fashion.

## Do not multitask since it is inefficient.

When you try to multitask it can end up costing you more than you would like it to. This creates an environment where you are forced to decide which task is more important than the other. For instance, while working on one task you may be distracted by another task, such as answering the phone. This can create anxiety around which one is more important at the time, such as finish the task you were working on or stop and answer the phone. These little decisions can cost you time and money in the long run. It can spend oxygenated glucose and cause you to lose the focus that you need. When you switch between tasks you are exhausting the effort you put into the original task and then becoming disoriented on how you are going to complete the current tasks on your list. Once you are engaged in working on one single task it is best to stay in that mode and continue with that task until you are completely done. When you do multitasking, you lose focus and it reduces your brains need to process the glucose you need.

## Limit your distractions from online interaction and emails.

By turning off your notifications you will be able to eliminate the urge to multitask which can create a cognitive inefficiency. This can also create memory issues as well as concentration abilities. The process of checking your email every few minutes while you are working can be distracting and also impair your decision-making skills. You should trick your brain into staying on a steady organized structured track of completing the work that you started with before moving on to another assignment. Turn off the notifications so that you will not be interrupted by pointless emails. If something is enormously important it will still be there when you are ready to check on it.

## First thing in the morning you will need to "eat the frog."

Start your day off right and as the day goes on you will be able to maintain that steady flow of positive energy throughout the day. Some of the most trivial questions that can block you up are the ones that pertain to nothing important. This can be anything from "Do I use a pen or pencil?" to "Which treatment method should I use for cancer?" Whatever choice you are trying to make you are using the same energy source to make those decisions, so make sure you maintain those energy storehouses. Important decisions are a necessary part of life and when faced with them you should do that first thing in the morning. By starting the day with a deep thoughtful decision-making process, it sets a tone for the rest of the day to be much easier. An old saying it can only get better from here rings true in this situation.

## Only excerpt the amount of time on a decision, activity, or task as that specific thing is worth.

To organize your bills and other important household documents you do not want to make it over complicated. The only time you should make a custom filing system is if you will be using those files on a daily basis. If it is something that you may not need for 5 years or more, then do not waste your time in organizing and decorating the compartment that you store it in.

## Utilize breaks often.

When you take breaks, you are allowing your mind to recharge and reset. This is a positive thing. As young children, we are taught to take naps, and at some point, in your childhood, you get away from taking naps—however, they are still quite beneficial to your health and your wellbeing. A small break or nap time is a great way to reboot during the day. These 15-minute breaks or naps will give your brain the chance to reset and build up some more energy for the rest of the day. A 15-minute break will increase the IQ and brain effectiveness by 10 points. That is a drastic increase when you consider what most people do with only 10% of their brain in the first place.

## Spend time in daydreams.

Since the brain operates in two separate oppositional modes which can be explained as simply the process of directing the thoughts and the process by which the thoughts will take over and then completely run themselves. When we are in directing mode, we will be able to get work done. This is utilized for any type of work that we do. Then when we are daydreaming we are allowing our thoughts to take over and then run themselves. This is the process by which a thought will meld into another thought and then it is controlled by the thought process so that they become a stream of thoughts creating an image that entertains. This mode will create a reset mode that helps your brain to replenish and then the neural button is able to replenish the glucose which helps with the tasks at hand. This helps to foster a great sense of creativity. This creativity will help you with your thought process and your imagination. It allows you to experience images and creative imagery.

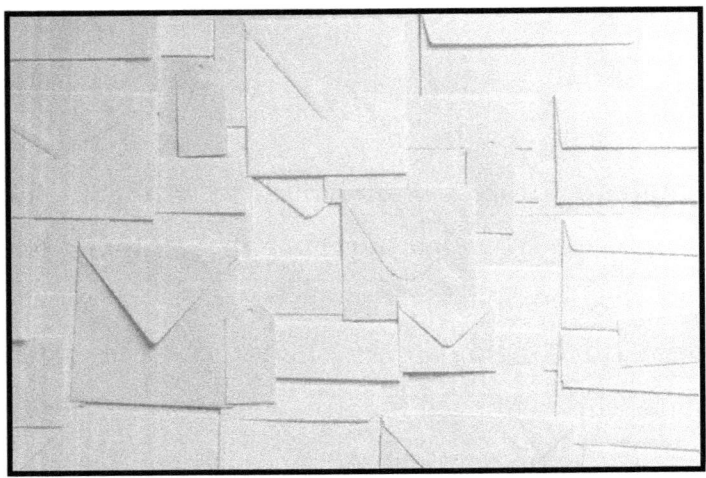

# Decluttering your social media usage

By using the handy chart which I have provided in the worksheet section of this book, you can get a good idea of the actual amount of time that you are spending on social media per day. Then you can examine which one you spend more time on. Once you have a clear pattern of behavior you can begin to eliminate the ones that you do not spend the most time using and work on decreasing the amount of time that you spend using that social media account during your day.

Now, let us imagine a social media timeline that you have already created for your social media activity and you can drastically change this schedule to fit your current needs. In this timeline, you might be using social media for 5 hours and 35 minutes on Monday. That seems like an awful lot of time on social media. So, let us look at the social media sites that you are using and the amounts of time that you are spending on these sites and devise a plan that would allow you to limit your time accessing them but still getting the most use from it. This will help to declutter your mind and social media usage and spend less time overwhelmed by it.

By eliminating a few of your social media accounts or scheduling to use your social media accounts only on specific days or between specific periods of your day you can begin to set a more manageable schedule for using social media. This will help you to reduce the clutter in your brain and eliminate the overwhelm that you feel from too much social media interaction. Later in this book, I will go over how you can schedule your day to better fit a calmer and peaceful day without stress and clutter.

## Clearing Out Your Email Inbox

By clearing your inbox each week, you can feel accomplished and confident that you are heading into a new week without baggage from the previous week. I have found that clearing my inbox on my email is a difficult task for me. I always worry that I will be deleting something I need or something that I will forget about, so instead of completely unsubscribing from all those emails I use Unroll.me and send the ones that I feel like I will miss to my roll up and the rest I unsubscribe to. This allows me to choose what to do with every single email that is coming into my email box. Once I figure out what emails I am eliminating then I can take that filter to my email box and delete all the emails from that email address out of my email inbox and storage. This helps me to only eliminate the ones that I genuinely want to clear out. It also allows me to drop my emails received in my email box down to the roll up and the ones that I kept in my inbox for a purpose.

# Uninstalling Software You Do Not Need

By uninstalling software that is not serving you a purpose anymore you are allowing space for new things to serve you in a better and more beneficial way. There are several apps that people tend to keep on their phones and these apps usually involve some social media. Through the use of the previous exercise to eliminate the overwhelm from your social media activity then you will be able to locate the apps that are no longer serving you in the best interest and begin to delete them from your life. For instance, I used to have Facebooks app on my phone. I would receive a ton of notifications and it would drain my battery. One day I decided that I had had enough of my battery on my phone being drained due to the Facebook app, which I hardly ever used, so I deleted it. I found that by deleting that simple app I not only freed up space within my phones hard drive, but I also freed up space in my own mind due to the release of all that clutter that came with Facebook. Now I am not saying I stopped using Facebook, however, I did notice a decrease in my use of Facebook after I deleted that app. I also found that I enjoyed the Instagram app much more and now I simply use that app more than I use Facebook.

Over time I have learned to use fewer apps on my phone. I started out with Facebook, Instagram, Pinterest, LinkedIn, Twitter, and StumbleUpon. Then over time, I found that I rarely used most of these apps. I deleted the ones that were not serving me, such as Pinterest, since I can log in on my browser and do the same functions. I also deleted twitter, since I never actually check it, and LinkedIn since I find no real use for that one. The first one I deleted was StumbleUpon, simply because I was not using it for anything but to follow other peoples content and this was creating more stress and clutter in my mind and my phone. Now my phone is streamlined and has limited amounts of apps that are unnecessary.

# Clearing the Junk on Your Phone

When you clean the junk from your phone you are freeing up space for more important things. Cleaning up junk is another way to get rid of the clutter that is banging around in your head. Cleaning your mind is a similar process as cleaning your phone. To clean your phone means that you are clearing out the old to allow room for the new. You are cleaning up the unwanted details that are blocking you from running at full capacity. You can also clean your mind in the same way.

When you clean your phone up you would do a cache clean up and eliminate the cached items that have been stored in your phone's storage system. Then you would identify the junk that is left over and remove it with a system app that allows you to remove the junk. Next, you will optimize the memory space that is being cleared up. To optimize the space means you are cleaning and checking for any tails of junk files that have not been cleaned by the cache or the removal program. Then by managing the apps and removing ones that you no longer use you can clear up more junk and space. Finally, you will remove any data that has been stored from ads.

This whole process, with a few modifications, can be utilized with your mind as well. By eliminating those memories that have been stored within your mind you can free up space for more memories that would be much more beneficial than the previous ones were. By allowing yourself to heal and rejuvenate you are eliminating the junk files that do not serve you. Then by taking a process of journaling, you can defragment all the negative and unnecessary files and memories that are holding your back. This is also another way to eliminate the clutter that has been overflowing in your brain and leaving you with a clear mind and a better way to feel healthy and capable to accomplish your tasks.

# Chapter 4: How Decluttering Can Improve Your Relationships

Up to this point, I have talked about what clutter can do for your life and how social media is influencing that clutter. In the rest of this chapter, I will talk about how clutter can hinder your relationships, increase your anxiety, and also limit your ability to make proper decisions. Cluttering up your mind is a difficult thing to break free form and it can create tons of problems in your life. If you are in a relationship with someone they may find you distant and uninterested in activities and spending time with them. This could be due to the stress that you are feeling from being overwhelmed with clutter.

# How Decluttering Can Improve Your Anxiety

When you declutter, you are clearing up those things that make you anxious and nervous. Studies have shown that by decluttering you can improve your health, as well as eliminate your anxiety.

Anxiety is intensified by the amount of clutter that is in your mind and your environment. By tossing things from your home that is no longer serving you will be able to reduce your anxiety with each item that you toss. The only thing that you need to remind yourself of every time you declutter your mind and your environment is that you are doing this to improve your health. If you do not have a clear goal in mind when you start you may end up reverting back to the cluttered mind and environment that you started with prior to the declutter.

To declutter you home environment and mind you should start with decluttering your attitude towards things. Ask yourself if these items are serving a purpose that is beneficial to your life. If you get a resounding no, then toss it out. This holds true for attitudes towards others and friendships, alike.

## Improving Your Attitude Towards Others In Your Life

To improve your attitude and thought processes you need to take stock of how you are responding to those around you.

- Do you respond in a negative way?
- Are you taking things in the wrong context?
- Did you think those actions thoroughly through?

These are all questions that need to be addressed when trying to edit how you respond to others and your thoughts. By examining how we respond to others and the attitude with which we present to the world we can begin to examine why we are this way and try to deviate from a negative attitude or thought process.

## Decluttering Your Relationships

Oftentimes, you will experience situations where you start to notice that some of your friends are really not that great. In this situation, you need to start to figure out the ones that are negative—and ultimately, eliminate them from your life. To start this process, you need to ask yourself a few simple questions.

## Who am I when I am around these friends?

Check in with yourself and identify who you are with and if they mesh with you properly. If you do not recognize who you are when you are around your friends, then it may be time to find new ones.

## What are these friends doing to help me with my positive outlook?

If you are questioning who you are and what type of person you have become while being around your friends, then they are not a positive influence. If they have you listening to music, you do not like or behaving in manners that are not appropriate then consider releasing them to find new friends.

**Is this behavior okay?**

Did you feel comfortable with the activities that you just did? Are you behaving in a way that would make your family mad at you? Did you think that your friend's behavior was inappropriate? If you have been struggling with the actions that others have taken, then you may want to reconsider hanging out with them.

**Disassociate with family and friends.**

Often times you find that you will need to disassociate with one or more family members. If this is the case, know that it will be hard. However, if they are not a positive influence in your life then you must cut them loose.

## Limit the associations that you have with family.

If you cannot completely cut them out of your life, then limit the amount of time that you spend with them. Disconnecting with friends and family that are not positive in your life will help to maintain your relationships that are positive and help to maintain your growth.

## Expand your friend list.

Find other people to hang out with. You will notice that the more you declutter your mind and your home, the less the old friends and family will connect with you. It is best to find new ones that fit into your life now as it is instead of hanging out with the ones that were with you prior to the growth and change.

# How to Identify a Bad Influence and Then Subsequently Illuminate Them

There are several archetypes of people that you will need to watch out for. I have listed just a few of these below. But the main thing to remember is that if the friendship is not serving you in a positive way, or you are continuously asking yourself "why am I friends with these people?" then you should consider letting the friendship go.

Many times, people will get comfortable in familiar situations such as friendships, housing environments, and the feeling of constant stress. Familiarity does not mean that it is the appropriate setting to be in, it simply means that you have changed your values and core beliefs to be comfortable in something that is not healthy. So, the next step in decluttering your life is to start to eliminate the things that are no longer serving you in life.

**Watch out for the opportunist.**

This is a person that is only out to get whatever they can from you. Look out for these character traits:

- Borrowing things from you may become a serious issue. They may ask to borrow money, without the intention of paying you back. They may try to borrow your clothing, as well as property, and they may never give those things back. Or, when they do return it the item is damaged. They might even allow other people to have your belongings, even though they did not ask if it was ok first.

- The continued probability that they will ask for a favor but not want to repay the favor ever.

- They only pay attention to you when you inform them

that you have something new and they are only interested in seeing it, so they can borrow it.

## Watch out for the self-centered person.

This is the all-about-me person—someone who only wants it to be about them. This would be narcissistic.

- They always have opinions about everything that involves others. An opinion is someone's ideas about their thoughts or feelings. It is not a fact. This is an assessment that they are making about something.

- A person that is self-centered will have no mind theory, they do not recognize empathy, and they fully believe everyone the same thing they do. This can be seen in younger children mostly.

- They do not separate their beliefs, or thoughts as well as ideas from other peoples. If you try to share the ideas that you have then this person will criticize or ignore you like you are not important.

**"Poor-me" person should be avoided.**

Stay clear of the victim mentality person, the one who exudes "poor old me," and "my life is so horrible."

- This person is needy and wants you to solve their problems. They are always needing advice. They always tell you how hard their life is. They will be mad at you even if they are in the wrong.

- They start stories with "Oh my god..." and "I can't believe...." They will often be found screaming "You do not understand the things that I am going through!" They crave attention all the attention and then steal all the spotlight at all times.

## Avoid clingy friends.

- This person does not like to share with others. They will be possessive of you and will not allow others to even hang out with you.

- They will want you to constantly be hanging out with you. They are often mad at you if you spend time together with other people.

## Keep the fake friend away.

- This is the type of friend that will be nice to the face and talk about you behind your back. They will stab you in the back and not think anything of it.

- They will sell you out to the first bidder. This friend will tell your secrets and expect you to not care.

- They like to pretend that they are your friend to get juice on you to spread to others.

- They will steal your friends by lying about your actions.

**Stay away from the snob**

- This person will think that their ethnicity is better than yours. They will consider themselves worthier of affection. They will think that they are a higher class than you or smarter than you.

- They will insult your heritage because it does not live up to theirs. This person will not appreciate anything you give them for birthdays of the holiday. They will turn their nose up and be too good for you.

**Do not keep the friend that ignores you.**

- This "friend" is absolutely infuriating to those that hang out with them. They will ignore your opinion on all things. They will ignore how you feel about every situation.

- They will find your thoughts boring and constantly blow you off when you talk. They will ignore your phone calls but expect you to answer theirs.

**Avoid the person that thinks they are queen bee.**

- This person is dominant and controlling. They must choose everything that you do. They control the look of the group.

- They will be the one that you have to check with when wanting to change something about you to make sure they will not be mad at you. They will make all the decisions for the group.

# Allowing Yourself To Cut Ties With Negative Influences

### Should you hold on to that friendship?

Decide whether you want to hold on to the friendship and whether it is worth continuing in the long run. Is the friendship really worth holding on to? Will this person be a more worthwhile friend in the end?

### Cease all contact with those that you wish to let go of.

If you are not going to continue to hold on to that friendship, then you should break all ties with them. Cease your contact with them and let them go on about their life.

## Inform the friend, when it feels appropriate, that your friendship is over.

If you are not able to quietly walk away and distance yourself from this friend, then you will need to talk with them when the timing is right and cease the friendship with them. The best option for a clean break up is to work out how to confront them face-to-face and inform them of the decision that you have made.

Breaking up with friends is hard, especially if they have been a major role in your life. But it is one thing that is necessary when you are dealing with toxic relationships. It is always best to break ties with people that are toxic in an environment that is warm and comforting. Somewhere that there will be no chance of a scene being caused, as well as the ability to have moral support.

If the person you are disconnecting yourself from is a family member then start slowly and limit your ties to them by spending less time around them. I have had to do this with several family members. If the person you are disconnecting from is toxic do not feel bad for letting them go, simply wish them well and limit your contact and exposure to them. However, do not avoid your favorite places or family members' homes because they are there, simply be cordial, acknowledge they are there and then make a clear exit from their personal space.

By eliminating the negative aspects in your life, you are able to start creating more positive changes that will have a bigger impact on your future. Do not feel shame for letting people go. Do not blame yourself for the failure of the relationship, simply acknowledge that the relationship has played its role in your life and now it is time to move forward.

# Chapter 5: Breaking the Habit of Multitasking And Alternatives for Stress Reduction

Reducing stress is a major aspect of decluttering your life and mind. Stress is a huge problem for many people on a daily basis and can create several health-related complications, as I discussed earlier. In this chapter I will go into more details about how stress can be reduced and what it will mean for your life. Multi-tasking is one way that many people create more stress in their lives. Below I have broken-down how stress and multi-tasking can affect even the most confident multi-tasker.

What is multitasking and how does it affect the habits and stress level of someone living with too much clutter in their mind? Multitasking is a great way to get more things done in a quicker time period. Or is it? Studies recently have shown the more you multitasking the more you are actually creating more stress than you are eliminating it. Believe it or not, multitasking is actually a less productive way to handle those things that you need to be doing as a single task process. As the study showed those that regularly bombard themselves with multiple electronics access for information are actually decreasing their ability to concentrate, pay attention, and worst of all recall the information that they have learned. If you find that you are switching from one job to another without completing either of them, then you should really consider eliminating multitasking form your lifestyle. One way that you can accomplish this is to complete one single task at a time.

Many people believe that they have a special knack for multitasking—however, research has shown that this simply is not possible. Many of those who believe in this multitasking trait is actually believing that the task helps their performance when in fact it is hurting them in the long run. They are not helping their situation any better if they would simply complete the same tasks but individually. The reason they performed so poorly at multitasking is due to the overwhelm and trouble they have with organizing the tasks at hand. Their thoughts would be cluttered with details that would prevent them from completing a task on time as well as completing any of the tasks at hand efficiently.

They also found that when switching from one task to another they would be much slower at completing the tasks and being able to switch their brain form one task to the next. This also proves true when you look at the efficiency of completions and performance during the task. The brain can only provide a focus for one single activity at a time. This means that the more items you include in your multitasking efforts the less any of them are completed to an efficiency that is needed for the performance that is expected. Your brain does not have the capacity to perform each individual task that is necessary for being successful for two tasks or more at once.

## Breaking the Habit of Multitasking

So how do you break the habit of trying to multitask? First, you need to understand that your neurochemistry is not working in your favor. But we can accomplish our same number of tasks that are needed to be accomplished when we tackle them one by one.

There are 5 specific steps that you can take to break through the multitasking urge.

1. Start this elimination of multitasking by taking an account of how often throughout the day you are getting distracted. This can be done by wining down any times that you had interruptions during meetings, as well as times that you got distracted while completing tasks. Examine what is distracting you and when it usually is happening. Then make a plan to block those distractions.

2. Turn your big tasks into bite-size chunks. The more bite-size chunks that you accomplish, the more confident you will be to complete the tasks at hand. You will be

more efficient with your results and accomplish more in a shorter amount of time.

3. Make sure you have eliminated all the distractions in your environment while working. If you tend to get multiple emails per day while working, then send an autoresponder that tells people that you are working on an important project and will get with them shortly. Also, set up a notification for any emails that are labeled urgent. Then get busy working on your tasks. This will allow you to avoid emails that could be distracting but not important.

4. Start each workday with 5 minutes of meditation and breathing exercises. This is a great way to calm the mind before the chaos of the day ensues. It also significantly allows you to decrease the distractibility of your mind during those work hours.

5. Consider shortening every single meeting to a 45-minute meeting instead of an hour meeting. Then you can adapt the difference in time for the meetings to a break that will allow you to check your email and catch up on the day's messages. Taking a mental break is another great way to get that much-needed recoup time during the day. You can also take that 15-minute time period to prepare for a more focused day with some exercise or mind focusing activities.

Changing your habits is always difficult. We are creatures of habit and anything you have been doing for a long time is now ingrained into your ways. However, it is entirely possible to change anything and everything you do not like about yourself or how you handle situations with a little bit of effort and spending the continuous effort to make it work. It only takes 21 days to make something habit that will eventually be a permanent characteristic. So, start slowly and push for those 21 days, at that time it should be instinctive and no longer something that you have to force yourself to do.

## A Few Key Steps to Consider When Changing Your Multitasking Ways:

Shift from multiple tasks to single tasks. This will allow your mind time to reboot between tasks and prevent you from burning out. Since your brain is the powerhouse to your body it needs time to recoup and replenish so giving it that time is essential to staying stress-free. Every couple of hours you should take a break and allow for 15-minutes of doing some replenishing or recouping activity. This can be a meditative session, or a power snack with lots of protein and vitamins.

### 1. Take a brain break when it is necessary.

By allowing your mind to reboot and recharge you are eliminating the clutter and overload that comes from too much information at one time.

To prevent a burn out you will need to accomplish your tasks I chunks. By blocking out time in your day that is work time and rest and recoup time, you are able to accomplish the things you need to each day without being overwhelmed, burnt out, or having too much clutter. Your brain needs to be replenished often and in order to do that you should have healthy snacks at hand for when you need a brain boost. Walnuts are a brain food, and protein such as beef jerky is a great source of energy and protein. Try incorporating some nut mixes into your midday snacks and using protein as a beginning of the day boost for your energy and brain power.

Now that I have given you lots of ways to help you with your urge to multitask I can begin to talk about how to use your time wisely. With less stress, you can accomplish more tasks. In order to succeed you will need to learn how to accomplish your tasks individually without added stress. Many people believe that by multitasking they can get more done, but they fail to realize that this is not helping them accomplish more it only looks that way. When each task is done at a performance level of average or below average they are simply not completing the tasks to the level that needs to be don and they are jeopardizing their work and job. So, a few key tasks that will help you to avoid performance levels being reduced by the multitasking urges is listed below.

## 2. Eliminate the things that are distracting you from completing your tasks.

Eliminate those things that distract you and lead you to multitask. Often times you may find yourself looking through your email while also handling another task, but this is not an ideal way to work. So, avoid checking email or social media while working. These things can lead to you being distracted and the work performance failing. You can eliminate these distractions by turning the email notifications off or turning your cell phone on silent.

## 3. Handle only one task at a time.

Earlier in this section address this but I would like to add to it that by doing one task at a time you are allowing yourself to be fully focused on that task. Use a blocking system to add time into your schedule for each task. In between the ending of one task and the starting of another task take time to journal the task that was completed and the task that is pending for completion by writing a short three sentence paragraph about what you just finished and then three more sentences about what you will be tackling next. This allows you to clear your mind of the task that you have finished and be fully focused on the task that you are jumping in to. This works really great at being able to complete a task fully before moving on to the next task. It also helps when breaking down a bigger task into small chunks to be completed in stages. You will have a record of each task that is completed so that you can review the process and know where you need to focus your time more efficiently at.

## 4. Re-training the brain to be completely in that moment is necessary.

The concept that came out a few years ago called "Be Here Now" focuses fully on this concept. By being present in the very moment that you are in and not focusing on the what-ifs or the future, as well as the past, you are able to have focused on the tasks at hand. Finding yourself at that moment will place you more intently on the task that you are completing and help you to accomplish more of the tasks that are needed to be accomplished at once. This concept will take some time to adjust to for those that are always multitasking or thinking of what they have to do tomorrow and what they did yesterday, but once you develop a pattern of being in the moment it will seem like second nature. Although the concept talks about being in the moment it does not mean that you do not plan for the future, such as vacations and bills, it simply means that you focus on what you can handle at this moment, not something that cannot be handled yet.

Listing to a podcast and driving to work is completely possible. However, if you are needing to focus on bath activities that you are accomplishing with a 98% or more accuracy, then the majority of people that are able to focus intently on two or more projects is less than 3%. That is a drastic difference than what many people consider their capabilities to be. Many times, I have been driving with the radio on and then suddenly I need to focus more intently to the road, so I find myself turning the radio off. This is due to the brains processing capabilities that is telling us that you will need your full cognitive capabilities to process the navigation of the road.

This rings true when working on projects at work. For instance, you may be browsing through some emails while you are in a meeting, but this presents a problem since know you have transferred the attention span to the emails and not the meeting. You may be actively present in the meeting, but you are not cognitively engaged with the meeting content. Another source of distraction that clutters up our brains and creates stress and chaos in our lives is our social media habits.

Multi-tasking in theory seems like a great way to get more done in your day, however, it simply creates more complications which leads to less focus and more stress. Below I have included alternative ways to eliminate that stress in your life so that you no longer feel like multi-tasking is the only way to get all your work done in your day.

## Exercise is another way to eliminate stress

By increasing your heart rate first thing in the morning you will be able to combat stress. Physical stress creates a relief system for mental stress. There are even more benefits to exercise than stress reduction. Those who exercise on a regular basis will have less stress than those who do not exercise as much.

The reasons that stress is reduced by exercise can be found listed below:

- It reduces the hormone that is related to stress, such as cortisol. Over time you will have fewer stress hormones and you will increase the release of endorphins which improves your mood and is a natural source for painkillers.

- Exercise has been known to increase your ability to sleep and improve the quality that you are getting. Stress affects your ability to sleep as well as the ability to have restful sleep that is rejuvenating. By exercising you increase your ability to rejuvenate and replenish through sleep.

- Confidence levels have shown a greater increase when people exercise. They feel more competent in their day jobs and their body and this, in turn, reduces their stress levels. By reducing the stress levels, they are able to improve their wellbeing and health.

Consider using an online app for exercise or doing some yoga, running, jogging, or cardio in the morning. You can incorporate rock climbing, running, jogging, walking, and other exercises into your daytime exercise routine. Using large muscle groups to exercise will increase your ability to elevate your stress reduction.

By gaining regular amounts of stress relief through exercise you are able to improve your health and overall declutter your mind.

## Use a candle.

Essential oils are a great way to relax the mind and de-stress. Scented candles are another great option. Below is a list of candles or essential oil scents that are a great way to de-stress or reduce your anxiety.

- Orange or orange blossom
- Roman chamomile
- Lavender
- Ylang ylang
- Rose
- Neroli
- Vetiver
- Geranium
- Sandalwood
- Bergamot
- Frankincense

The method of using scents or essential oils to calm your mind is call aromatherapy. Studies have proven the effectiveness of aromatherapy to decrease your stress and anxiety levels as well as improve your sleeping habits.

**Stop drinking caffeine.**

Caffeine is a substance that stimulates your energy. This can be quite dangerous in high dosages. They can increase your anxiety levels and cause you more problems in the long run. It is simply a good idea to stop drinking caffeine.

**Chew some gum.**

By chewing gum, you can have a super and quick way to reduce your stress. Studies have shown that gum is a great way of offering a sense of well-being and lower your stress levels. The only explanation to this would be that gum creates brain waves which are similar in relaxed people. Another reason is that by chewing gum you are increasing the blood flow to your brain.

## Spend time with loved ones.

Being social will increase your sense of belonging, and self-worth. It will decrease your stress and allow you to have a more positive connection with yourself and other people. For women, they have found that when they spend time with children they release oxytocin which naturally relieves stress. this is the opposite effect of fight and flight and it is called tend and befriend.

## Laugh often.

It is super hard to be anxious and stressed when you are laughing aloud. To laugh aloud you will have good health, as well as be able to relieve stress.

- Stress release.
- Tension release and relaxation of muscles.
- Improve your immune system
- Improve your mood

It is highly known that the happier you are the less stressed you are. This is directly connected to your ability to accomplish more work throughout your day. Those that love what they do will accomplish more in their day and life than those that stress about it all day or hate the work that they are doing.

**Say "NO" more often.**

Sometimes stressors will be out of your control. Take an active part of your life and be in control of the things that you can change. This will also reduce your stress levels. If you say no more often you will be able to reduce the overwhelm that you would feel from constantly agreeing to things.

When you constantly agree to extra tasks that should be accomplished by the person asking you, you create more stress and a need to multi-task. This is not a healthy way of living. By creating more activities and responsibilities in your life and day you are ultimately setting yourself up for failure and overwhelm. Eventually you will crash and it will be hard.

## Avoid the procrastination bug.

Stay on top of all of those prioritize that are in your life and do not procrastinate. Procrastination can make you reactive and lead to a scrambling for you to catch up on things that are more important. When you scramble to catch up you end up more stressed and this can affect your sleep and health. Make a to-do list in order to organize your goals and priorities. Set realistic deadlines and goals and work your way down your list until you have accomplished the things that you were wishing to accomplish. Work on things that are necessary for today and chunk out time that is uninterrupted for those things that need to be done at a later date.

**Practice mindfulness.**

I spoke of this earlier, but a practice of mindfulness or meditation can reduce anxiety, and help you feel less stressed. This is a simple process to practice. It takes as little as ten minutes per day to practice mindfulness or meditation.

Ten minutes per day has been known to reduce stress, clear the mind, open up new channels of communication with your own body and have more creative imagination. This creates a more productive work day and also helps you to eliminate the need to multi-task.

**Practice deep breathing.**

Take 5 minutes out of each day to practice a deep breathing exercise. Sit up straight in your chair and breath in deep placing a hand on your belly and inhaling deeply. Then as you exhale feel the difference in your stomach. Feel your breath begin to exhale into your abdomen and work all the way through your lungs to your stomach. Allowing the breath to completely encompass your body. Then releasing it slowly and systematically.

**Cuddle with someone that you love.**

Cuddles increase your mood by positive physical contact. It releases oxytocin and then lowers cortisol. This will lower your blood pressure as well as your heart rate. These are all physical manifestations of stress. Humans are not the only ones in the world who thrive on cuddles. Dogs will cuddle, so will many other animals in the animal kingdom.

**Music is a great way to relieve stress.**

When you listen to music you will feel relaxed and more at peace. This will lower your heart rate and help induce a relaxation mode that will help you sleep and also calm the stress. It lowers blood pressure, stress hormones, and heart rate.

**Interact with your pet.**

Pets can be extremely helpful to your health. They can help to improve our mood and also reduce stress. To interact with a pet will help release oxytocin which helps to promote your positive moods. Pets can also prolong your lifespan and keep you active by providing you with a daily purpose.

**Reach out to others.**

Reach out to those on social media who have similar interests, as well as those that can help you with dealing with your stress. Talk to those that will provide assistance or moral support.

## Connect with your body.

Take a mental stroll through your body and get a clear sense of what is affecting your body at this time. Examine the stress levels within your arms and legs. Check to see if you have stress in your shoulders or back. Make sure you identify the stresses in your life.

## Take time to decompress.

Decompressing will help you with your stress levels. Use a warm wrap around your neck for 10 minutes and close your eyes. This is a technique that many spa centers use to help you relax.

Taking time to decompress can mean anything from reading a book, to a brisk walk in the park. Whatever your favorite decompressing activity is make sure to incorporate it into your day so that you can rejuvenate your mind, body, and soul with positive light and energy.

**Show gratitude.**

Using your journal that we talked about in another chapter will help you to appreciate the things that you have that are positive in your life. This can be done by inserting gratitude into the journal that you are already creating with the steps in this book.

**Watch what you eat and drink.**

Alcohol as well as unhealthy food can abuse your body and may seem to help with lowering your stress levels, but this is far from the truth. It actually adds to it.

**Be more assertive.**

Do not force yourself to meet the expectations of others it is simply not necessary. You can say "No" to others when they request you to do things that you do not want to do. When you are being assertive this will allow you to have the courage to stand up to others for your right to be who you are and hold the belief that you have, however it still shows them respect for their beliefs.

## Stop smoking and any other bad habits.

Apart from the health risks of smoking, nicotine can be a stimulant which will bring you more stress and that is not what you need. Reward yourself with the rewards that you earn from dropping unhealthy habits.

## Exercise on a regular basis.

Choose a non-competitive exercise activity and set goals that are reasonable. Aerobics is a great way to release endorphins which increases your energy and lowers stress.

## Relaxation techniques should be studied and practiced regularly.

Relaxation is needed every day. Choose multiple techniques to practice a relaxation technique. Blend them together and get a mix of both relaxation and aerobics to find a surefire way to provide your whole body with stress-reducing effects.

## Take responsibility for your actions.

Control the things that you can and then leave the things that you cannot alone and do not let them stress you out. By taking responsibility for your own actions you are able to let go of the stress that you feel from holding on to revenge, neglect, fear, and shame that comes from others actions or your own. Allow yourself to only take on your own responsibility in your own actions and your own life. Release the ones that are not yours and forgive those that have harmed you, just never forget.

## Reduce things in your life that stress you out.

Many people notice different things in their life that stress them out. By reducing these things, they can avoid the stress that would normally come from those stressful things. If that new class is to stressful then consider taking it at a time that is less stressful in life. If you are dealing with things in life that are adding extra, unnecessary stress in your life, then let them go.

## Live by the values that you set.

The more you follow your belief system, the better you will feel. The better you will feel about yourself, the less stress you will feel. When you use your values to frame your life you will feel better about your life.

Values are what makes up who we are. They are the code by which we live by. If you fail to follow your own values you will find that your life is more cluttered and you feel more stress day to day.

## Make sure your goals are realistic and achievable.

You cannot guarantee that you will 100% reach a goal that you set but the more realistic the goal the better chance you will have. If your goals are not realistic then how do you expect to accomplish them. If at this time the goal you have set is not realistic but with work, it can be then start at the bottom and reward yourself for every single step forward. This will help you to create a guide book of how to accomplish these goals that did not seem so realistic prior to starting.

## Love yourself unconditionally.

When you experience episodes of overwhelmed, remember who you are and remind your subconscious that you are a great person that does well. Your self-esteem should be healthy and confident. No matter what you have done in life you are a unique and beautiful person. Love you for who you are and what you have been through. Without unconditional love you cannot move forward.

# Chapter 6: Relieve Stress By Eating Healthy, Adding Healthy Habits And Utilizing Meditation

Meditation can be a great stress reliever. When you meditate you are teaching yourself how to calm what many Yogis call the "Monkey Brain." "Monkey Brain" is that overactive, constantly thinking brain that most of us have. When you are over thinking the situations in your life, or you are experiencing overwhelm and chaos then you should consider sitting down and meditating.

Many people think that meditating is a process by which you clear your mind and they often think that it is not something they will be able to do. But this is simply not true. Meditating is the process of acknowledging your thoughts and then letting them move on from the space within your mind that they are occupying.

By utilizing meditation, you can begin to clear your mind over time by a process of acknowledging the thoughts and feelings that are blocking you from moving forward and then allowing them to be released into the world. Meditation can be utilized in several different ways. You can do a walking meditation, a seated meditation, and even a guided meditation. Below I have included a simple meditation practice that you can incorporate into your daily practice to help center and focus you.

## Breathing Exercises That Work

To start meditating you will need to learn a simple breathing technique. Most people would be surprised to know that they are not properly breathing. To breath properly you should start by breathing into one nostril and then out the other nostril slowly. As you practice this you can move on to breathing into one nostril, holding that breath for the count of 4 and then breathing out of the other nostril slowly.

Each time you breathe in you will need to breathe in so deep that you can feel it in your throat, chest, lungs, and then stomach. You need to breathe into your body all the way down to your feet. Then as your release that breath you should breath out slowly allowing the breath to escape your body and lungs in a slow and methodical way. After practicing a few of these breathing techniques you will be able to utilize this technique for calming exercises and even meditation.

## Weekly Meditation

*Breathing in deeply*
*Holding it for 4 seconds*
*Breathing out slowly*

*Breathing in deeply*
*Holding it for 4 seconds*
*Breathing out slowly*

*Breathe in the calm peaceful air*
*Breathe out tension and stress*

*Breathing in deeply*
*Holding it for 4 seconds*
*Breathing out slowly*

*Breathe in relaxation and peace*
*Breathe out releasing of negativity and chaos*
*Breathing in deeply*
*Holding it for 4 seconds*
*Breathing out slowly*

*Breathe in feeling that air going all the way to your feet*
*Breathe out tension and all the stress that you hold there*
*Breathing in deeply*
*Holding it for 4 seconds*
*Breathing out slowly*

*Breathe in feeling that air going all the way to your legs*
*Breathe out tension and all the stress that you hold there*
*Breathing in deeply*

*Holding it for 4 seconds*
*Breathing out slowly*

*Breathe in feeling all that air going to your hips*
*Breathe out stress and all the tension that you are holding there*
*Breathing in deeply*
*Holding it for 4 seconds*
*Breathing out slowly*

*Breathe in the air all the way to your spine letting it uncoil*
*Breathe out pain and suffering that you are feeling within your spine*

*Breathing in deeply*
*Holding it for 4 seconds*
*Breathing out slowly*

*Breathe in the air deep to your shoulders and let your shoulders relax*
*Breathe out no more weights weighing on your shoulders and release it*

*Breathing in deeply*
*Holding it for 4 seconds*
*Breathing out slowly*
*Breathe in white light through the top of your head coming down from above*
*Breathe out slowly and release all of your tension, stress, chaos, and fears*

*Breathing in deeply*
*Holding it for 4 seconds*
*Breathing out slowly*

*Breathe in white light washing over your body healing all those areas that you just breathed live and air into*

*Breathe out healed and rejuvenated*
*Breathing in deeply*
*Holding it for 4 seconds*
*Breathing out slowly*

# Making healthier food choices can help eliminate stress and overwhelm

## Healthy Eating Choices

Healthy meal choices involve:

- No Trans Fat
- Fruits
- Lean protein
- vegetables
- Less sugar

Nutrition is a big part of being healthy. Below is a detailed list of healthy foods and what they add to your diet. In order to be stress-free, you must be healthy. Berries, as well as fruits, are a popular health food that many people enjoy through the year. They also taste incredible. Fruits can be extra healthy for those that eat them fresh or raw. They contain high levels of vitamins and minerals as well as antioxidants. There are many fruits that can be used for increasing your nutrients. These include:

## Apples

Apples are a high fiber fruit that is loaded with lots of vitamin c, as well as numerous antioxidants. They are a filling snack and great for being added to pies, breakfast meals, toppings on meals, as well as a wonderful side dish.

## Avocados

Avocados are a high vitamin C type fruit that has recently been brought into mainstream media due to the popularity they have among health enthusiasts. They are high fat, low carb., and high fiber fruits that taste delicious as slices on toast, in a dip, and in dressings. They can have a creamy and rich taste that makes for a wonderful addition to any meal.

## Banana

Bananas are extremely high in fiber as well as potassium, which makes for a wonderful fruit for bowel health and muscle health. They provide a portable way to get several vitamins such as vitamin b6, and they make for an easy and effective way to snack throughout the day with very little waste or trash.

## Blueberries

Blueberries are a delicious fruit that can be found on vines throughout the country. They grow wild and are sweet to taste. They provide you with the antioxidants you need to fight cancer cells, as well as provide you wonderful topping for ice cream, cereal and pop able snacks.

## Oranges

Oranges are so high in vitamin C that they are the go-to fruit for people when they start to feel sick of weak during the winter months. They are great for juicing and provide lots of fiber, which is good for bowel health. They are high in antioxidants which is a great cancer fighting nutrient that is needed to stay healthy. For a great portable snack with biodegradable packaging take an orange with you to work or school and experience more energy and added health benefits.

## Strawberries

Strawberries are high in nutrients that we need such as, vitamin C, manganese, fiber, and low in carbs which makes them a highly nutritious food. They are delicious to eat and add to any dessert as well as being a low-calorie topping.

## Other Healthy Fruits

These are only a few fruits that can be used to be healthier in life. Below is an additional list of fruits that will be great additions to any diet plan.

- Cherries
- Pineapples
- Plums
- Pears
- Grapes
- Grapefruit
- Peaches
- Kiwi
- Olives
- Raspberries
- Melons
- Lemons
- Mango

Protein is an important aspect to any meal. In order to maintain higher levels of energy every day you will need to incorporate lots of protein into your diet. There are several ways to do this. One way is to get protein form animals an animal by-product such as eggs, meat, and dairy. The second way to get protein is to eat legumes and other vegetables that are high in protein. Below is a listing of the types of proteins that are available to you and how they help your body maintain it s health so that you feel less stress and more energy.

## Eggs

Eggs are the most nutritious option for breakfast meals. They are not loaded with sugar like cereals are and they provide tons of cholesterol that is good for your heart health. They are a safe food to eat daily when paired with the healthy bread option and some turkey bacon. When you need that early morning protein boost consider a boiled egg and some beef jerky. Try adding some boiled eggs or scrambled eggs to your favorite salad for some added protein and fiber.

## Meats

Nutritious foods that are healthy and unprocessed. Meat can be a great source of protein and added nutrients. Cooking meat gently can intensify the vitamins and nutrients.

## Lean Beef

Great source of proteins and lean fat. Also loaded with bioavailable iron. Low carb and fatty cuts are great for a low carb diet.

## Chicken Breasts

Chicken is one of the leaner meats that you can eat, however by choosing a fattier cut of the chicken you can gain a healthy addition to your low carb diet. They provide a large portion of the healthy fats that you need for sustaining your energy as well as provide you with a great source of nutrients while being low in calories and high in protein.

## Lamb

Lamb is one of the cleanest meats since it is grass-fed. This provides a much oiler skin and coat which provides you a high content of Omega-3 fatty acids when prepared properly. The meat of a lamb that is grass fed is more flavorful and healthier than any other meat source. It is a wonderful source of protein and tastes great.

## Peanuts, Nuts, and Seeds

These are an amazing option for losing weight, higher nutrients and vitamins as well as protein. Nuts are extra crunchy as well as fulfilling which makes them a great snack or topping choice for a salad. They are high in the nutrients that you need for a healthy body. These include vitamin E and magnesium. To prepare them you will simply open them and start snacking. This helps make them an easy snack to incorporate into your diet.

## Almonds

Almonds are a great addition to a salad or trail mix. They are loaded with antioxidants, vitamin E, fiber and magnesium. Scientists know that almonds are a great source for losing weight and they also contain helpful metabolic health benefits which are quite impressive.

## Chia Seeds

Chia seeds provide a high quantity of nutrients and one single ounce can contain over 11 grams of fiber. They also contain the daily requirement of manganese, calcium, magnesium and several other nutrients.

## Coconuts

Coconuts have a high content of fiber that provides a powerful amount of the essential fatty acids which are aptly names triglycerides which are medium-chain.

## Macadamia Nuts

Macadamias are extremely tasty and contain a higher monosaturated fat content as well as a lower omega-3 fatty acids content. This makes them a healthy nut to add to your meals.

## Walnuts

Walnuts are nutritious with all sorts of fiber vitamins that provide the daily nutrients that you need to be healthy.

## Peanuts

Peanuts, which are actually legumes have an incredible taste as well as a high content of antioxidant and nutrients. A scientist has found that peanuts provide a great weight loss food for healthy dieters. As long as you are not allergic. However, peanut butter can be highly fattening so take it easy.

## Vegetables

Vegetables provide thousands of vitamins and minerals that can be a great addition to any meal. Just make sure you only use fresh or frozen vegetables. There are tons of vegetables that are available in the supermarkets today and you should indulge in a variety of them every single day.

## Broccoli

Broccoli, which is a cruciferous vegetable, has a great taste and is good for you when both cooked and raw. Broccoli is loaded with fiber, Vitamin C, Vitamin K, and protein which makes this vegetable great for snacking and meal planning.

## Carrots

The carrot, which is a root vegetable, is an extra tasty, crunchy vegetable that full of all the fiber and nutrients that you need to stay healthy and full. They are loaded with vitamin K, carotene, and antioxidants for several health benefits.

## Cucumber

We all know the cucumber. It is great in our salads and super delicious as a pickle. They are low-calorie snacks that have minimal carbs. This is due to the high content value of water in them. They do contain nutrients in small amounts to include Vitamin K.

## Garlic

Garlic is a wonderful source of allicin, as well as bioactive compounds that have many biological effects that are quite powerful. This can increase your immune functions as well as provide a ton of other benefits.

## Kale

Kale has been found to be delicious and healthy. They have lots of vitamin C, vitamin K, as well as fiber. These provide you with nutrients that are a great health benefit. They provide a wonderful and crunchy snack as well as a healthy addition to a sandwich or salad.

## Other Healthy Vegetables

The list above only provided you with a few vegetables that are healthy, below I have listed several more:

- Swiss chard
- Artichokes
- Brussels sprouts
- Mushrooms
- turnips
- Cabbage
- zucchini
- Radishes
- Celery
- Eggplant
- Squash
- Leeks

- Lettuce

**Seafood**

Seafood is one of the healthiest foods that you could eat. They are loaded with lots of nutrients, as well as omega-3 fatty acids, and iodine, which is necessary for your body to be healthy. Scientists have shown that those that enjoy mostly fish as their meat source have been living longer as well as a lower risk of heart disease, depression, and dementia.

**Salmon**

Salmon has tons of omega-3s due to the higher content of oil on their skins. They are also highly loaded with nutrients and vitamin D.

**Sardines**

Sardines although small, have an oily texture that is providing you with lots of omega-3 fatty acids.

They also contain large quantities of nutrients that are needed for a healthy mind and body.

**Shellfish**

Shellfish are a great source of nutrients, which make them a healthy choice above other food groups. It is a shame that few people indulge in shellfish, even though they should. There nutrition level is on par to the level of the organ meats and the density is nutrient. Edible shellfish can be considered clams, oysters, and mollusks.

**Shrimp**

Shrimp is high in vitamin B12 and provides you with large quantities of nutrients. They also provide you will selenium which is a great nutrient for your body.

**Grains**

Although they have been deemed bad in the past few years, they can be a great source of fiber.

There are few that are healthy and low in carbs. However, most grains are high in carbs and not a popular food if on the paleo diet. The problem is you cannot just lump all grains together. Some are healthier than others. However, you need to be aware that they do have higher levels of carbs.

**Brown Rice**

Rice, which is a staple food for most of the world, is used in cereal as well. Brown rice, which is whole grain, is nutritious and contains large amounts of fiber, magnesium, and vitamin B1.

**Oats**

Oats can be a healthy choice for breakfast. They are full of fiber which is called beta-glucans, and nutrients that are shown to be highly healthy.

**Quinoa**

Quinoa is a great side choice for those individuals that are health-conscious. This tasty grain is full of magnesium and fiber. They also have lots of plant-based protein.

## Bread

Bread is one of the most popular items on the dinner plate, and that is why many people eat tons of it. However, bread is not healthy. It is high in carbs.

## Ezekiel Bread

Ezekiel bread one of the healthiest bread that the grocer will have. Made from whole grains that are sprouted, organic, and full of several legumes.

## Dairy

There are many lactose intolerant people in the world and those that are lactose intolerant are not missing out on anything. However, the people that can tolerate milk or lactose are found to be healthier as well as have a lesser chance of obesity and diabetes 2. The full-fat milk is high in calcium as well as other bioactive fatty acids similar to CLA.

## Cheese

Cheese is extremely nutritious and comes in a bite-size packaging. Each slice contains the same nutrients of a cup of milk. Cheese is also delicious and nutritious.

## Whole milk

Whole milk has a large number of minerals, vitamins, healthy fats, and animal protein. Whole milk provides lots of calcium.

## Yogurt

Yogurt, fermented milk with probiotics cultures is a great source of probiotics as well as nutrients.

Yogurt provides some of the same benefits as a glass of milk.

**Fats and Oils**

Many people are using fats and oils today for deep frying, cooking, basting, and preparing meals in other ways. This is not your old school fats and oils either. This is a new generation of fats and oils.

Each one of these delicious foods provide you with a wide range of added nutrients and vitamins that will help to replenish the nutrients and vitamins that you will be missing by your body processing stress. When you stress your body and overwhelm your senses you can begin to lose nutrients and vitamins that are an essential part of growing and being healthy. Without proper nutrients you will not sleep well, you will make poor choices, and you will find yourself living in a state of chaos and clutter due to the inability to focus your mind.

# Chapter 7: Decluttering Your Thoughts By Keeping A Journal

Journaling is an effective way to manage the clutter within your brain and also a great way to help you to decompress and de-stress. I utilize a journaling procedure that allows me to journal all of my necessary thoughts for the day. I sit down and write the date on the top of the page and then proceed to write every single thought that I have that is floating through my head. I start with what I call a brain dump and then I work towards a process of gratitude as well as answering questions that will help me to reduce the stress that is happening in my life. A few of those questions can be found below.

Anytime during the day that you are feeling overwhelmed, cluttered or stressed sit down with your notebook and pen and begin to journal those thoughts onto paper. If you are not positive about what you should write, then below I have included several journals prompts to help you with this process.

## Stress-Reducing Journal Prompts:
**Purge**

Purge your every thought and feeling. Start by writing what you are feeling, and then go into your thoughts, and then just let it flow. Whatever is bothering your or even the positives that have happened that day. It does not matter what your journal is about in this process as long as you are placing it on paper and not holding it in your mind. When you store all these things inside your mind you are taking up valuable space that can be used for other things. Once you have released it, you are able to give yourself the permission that you need to leave it in the journal. This allows you to free up that space that was being blocked by worry, anger, upset, and overwhelm.

**Journal Prompts to Get You Started**

Start with "Right now, I wish...." And finish the sentence. Fill in as many details about what you wish for right at this very moment. You can do this is several ways with several different sentences, such as:

"I wish I had..."
"I want to...."
"If I had..."
"What would happen if..."
"Where would I be if...."
"What can I do about...."

And so on. Each one creates a lead into for a new and exciting journal entry that will help clear the clutter.

## List your accomplishments.

Sit down with pen in hand and begin to list all the things that you have accomplished in your life. Write down the victories that you have had with work, schooling, family, and friends. List those things that were super small and those that were super huge. Just start to list them like you were being introduced to someone that would love to know all of these amazing things about you.

## Meditative Journaling

Take the time to sit quietly and concentrate on all the things that you feel inside your body. Concentrate on the breath going in and out of your lungs and before you start to journal take that time to really focus deep into your body and mind. Then pick up the pen and let it all flow.

Listening to your body will help you connect with the insides and feel the strength, the weaknesses, the healthy, the unhealthy that is within your body and you will be able to get valuable insight and character analysis about yourself through this process. You will be able to identify what is making you stronger, what is making you stressed, where the clutter is coming from and how to eliminate it.

**Heart-To-Heart With Your Mind**

Sit down and place pen to paper allowing yourself to talk freely inside your head. Journal all the things that you are telling yourself. Journal all the dismissive things that your inner critic is telling you about you. Let them come out and then dismiss them and reframe them in a positive and more uplifting way. Tell your inner critic that you will not hear that mess anymore and that you are stronger and wiser now. Allow the inner critic to reply telling you the things that you are not doing right and respond back with positive ways that you are leading your life. Make not of the positives. Allowing yourself to journal only the good that comes from this activity. In the end, you should have a positive rule book to live by.

## Positive Word of the Day

Decide on one positive word for the day and write it down. Then focus intently on using that word to the best of your ability all day. These positive words can be words such as:

- Gratitude
- Compassion
- Love
- Joy
- Courage
- Strength
- Radiance
- Enthusiasm
- Adventurous
- Enigmatic

Use one word per day to journal all the things that you exhibit in your character and how you show this positive word to the world. Then each day, use that word to frame your day with and share that word with the word through actions and character.

## Choose one situation that causes anxiety, and write it out.

Choosing one situation that is causing you great anxiety get your pen and notebook and begin to journal about that situation. Write down all the details about it and what is causing you so much stress. Ask questions that will lead to a deeper understanding of what it is that is bothering you and why you can't seem to get past it. Be supportive in your writing and encourage your inner mind to work out the details and solve the problem before you get up. Try to use complete honesty when it is necessary. This is the only way that you will be able to complete this journal prompt. Look at the problem from an angle that you have not already used to examine it by. This will help you to move forward with the problem and provide a solution that you never thought off.

## Write about something you love to do that improves your mindset.

Consider an activity that you love to do that provides improvements to your mindset. Sit down and write out activities that you would enjoy doing right now or one that has shown great improvement to your mindset and stress levels. How did this activity change your life for the better? What type of activity is this? How do you feel after completing this activity? What would you change if you could be involved in this activity more often? Make sure that the activity that you are writing about is a positive healthy one.

## Tell your story.

We all have a story. You know, that one story that we tell people to show that we have made a difference in the lives of others. Yes, that story. What did you think I was talking about the other type of story? No that is not for this book. This story is the one that makes you seem like a hero. The story that when you need a pick me up you go back to that and say I helped someone in need. Sit down with pen in hand and author this story. Talk about how you changed the person's life and created a better outlook for them. Tell how you helped them accomplish a goal of achievement. Tell how you saved that baby kitten for the little girl. Whatever your story is tell it in your own words on paper. This will provide you a way to feel more connected to the story and also offer you an uplifting story to read later when you are feeling less than hero-like. '

## Write about activities that you could do to feel complete joy and happiness for a whole day.

With pen in hand sit down and journal about all the things that you wish you could do in one day that would make you feel joy, happiness, and fulfillment. Free-writing the list of ideas that would serve you in a momentous way is a great thing to include in a weekly journal entry. Consider the activities that you can incorporate into your day form the time your rise till the time that you lay your head down at night. This can be anything that makes you engaged, excited about life, or fulfilled. Then every morning prior to getting out of bed examine this list and pick one item off the list to work towards. You can either do it that day or you can begin planning for it if it is something that will be large or extravagant.

## Start journaling by answering a few questions:

1. What is the feeling you wish to feel every day when you wake up?

2. What five things do you want to incorporate in your day today?

3. What five things would you want to incorporate into your future days?

4. Do you already feel stress or anxiety about today? What activity can you add to today's to-do list that will decrease these stressors?

5. What one thing can you improve upon your daily activities or life, such as communication improvements, time management, daily schedule improvements, less social media time, and other things?

6. Name one adjustment that you can change about your morning routine?

7. Name one change that you can make to your nightly routine?

8. Name one emotional trigger that you can let go of today?

9. Make a list of ten-twenty things that make you extra happy.

10. Write your favorite song lyrics to a song that makes you overjoyed. Then analyze why this song is the one that you chose?

11. Where is the one place that you wish you could travel to? And what makes you love it so much?

12. Name one way that you have been using patience with other people in your life? If not, how can you?

13. What new skill or training would you like to learn? In what way can you accomplish this?

14. What areas in your life could you be more organized than you are currently? What would it take to accomplish this? How can you prevent this area of your life form getting cluttered up again in the future?

15. Name one goal that is long-term which you can start to work towards right now?

16. Using your imagination draw something that makes you genuinely happy. Then,

write a paragraph or two on that image and why it makes you happy.

17. Write in detail the steps that you have taken to advance you towards your goals whether short term or long term?

18. What additional steps can you take this very moment to push you further towards your goal?

19. What steps could you incorporate into your daily life to begin a long-term goal?

20. Name the one thing that scares you to death about doing. Then write how you can use that fear to overcome it and do it anyways.

21. In what way can you be much more mindful of other people?

22. What made today much more difficult than any other day? What can you do to prevent

this same situation from happening in the future?

23. Name one problem that you handled today and how you handled it. Then journal about whether or not it was the best way to solve that problem.

24. What ways are you taking to incorporate self-care into your daily routine? Have you been allowing yourself the proper amount of time to heal and recuperate? If not, then in what ways can you change that and make your life much better?

25. Consider a mistake that you have made in the past and how you would handle it today. What was the lesson that you learn from this mistake and how could you utilize that lesson in the future?

26. What is one thing that scares the heck out of you?

## Stress Journal

These questions I utilize in my stress journal. A stress journal is a way to monitor the levels of stress that I am experiencing on any given day. It allows me to get a larger picture of what is truly bothering me and then use that information to correct those emotions or stressful situations. I start by asking just a few questions and then I move on to a plan for eliminating the stress that I have identified.

- Examine your body and really concentrate on the shoulders, lower back, neck, and stomach area. How does the worry as well as anxiety that you are carrying affect the stress response in the body?

- Look for tension, aches, pain, and tightness. Where are these located within your body?

- When you are dealing with stress, what

phrase could you say to yourself that would help you recognize and then handle the stress you are dealing with? This can be a simple mantra or affirmation.

- What affirmation resonates with how you feel right now?

- What stress have you been keeping to yourself and could easily be helped by telling someone else?

- When you examined the stress in your body what did you feel or connect with?

- How can you be more aware of your stress levels?

- How can you better handle your stress management?

- What mantra can you incorporate into your day to handle your stress?

- Name a relevant situation that took place which has created the stress?

- Was the stress that was created a warranted response?

- Did I blow that situation out of proportion to the real situation?

- Did I have full control of the situation?

- Did that situation involve someone else that was instrumental in the stress?

- Was there contribution warranted to the situation?

## Use your journal and write down that "head trash."

Write down the trash that is cluttering up your head. Write down the mean things that come up when you are doing self-talk. Those things that make you hate yourself when you are in that negative mood and are trash talking yourself. However, reframe that conversation with a different dialogue. Reframe it to be more positive and less aggressive. Find a way to change what you are saying to something much more positive.

- Consider why negative trash talk is the first thing that comes to you when something goes wrong.

- Why is the conversation within your head the one that makes you feel horrible about yourself?

- Why is negativity the very first thing that pops up?

Look in the mirror and think of all the things that you say to yourself that is negative and condescending. Then, consider the positives that you see in yourself while you are standing there looking in the mirror. Consider the way that you alter the negative to mean a positive.

We are all living in a sort of storyline and within that storyline is the actions and adventures that we take throughout our lifetime. Often times we will forget that we are authoring our own storyline and we begin to feel down about our life and what has taken place in it. However, we have the ability to edit and change this. We can create a whole new storyline.

**Examine the clutter in your home, and ask yourself how you feel inside about it.**

Once you create your Head Trash list, examine the space and take note of the words that you say to yourself in those moments. Consider that there are times that you may not get things done and that is ok. Not everything has to be accomplished sometimes it may take you a week to put the sheets back on the bed or to hang those new curtains. There may be a subconscious reason you have not placed those sheets on or put a curtain up. Consider what the subconscious reasons would be and then examine why that reason is the way it is. Think about what has made you hold this belief.

When you declutter your space, it will only work if you are aware of what you expect the end result to be. This is the time that you should sit down and consider what you want your space to look like and then begin the process of decluttering and shaping that environment. By decluttering your space, you will start to declutter your mind, but you have to be specific to what you want and how you will get there.

**Be in the present.**

It is not necessary for you to purchase a bulk supply of that household cleaner or stock up on can goods for an apocalyptic disaster. Sometimes it is much better to be present and in the moment. Often times people that are living in clutter will find it compulsory to purchase larger quantities of overstock food or supplies for an incase moment that could happen later on in the future. This event that compels them to purchase large amounts of supplies may never come but they will be fully prepared for it if it does happen.

So instead of being compulsive with your purchases and creating more clutter in your environment, it is best to stay present at the moment. Do you need ten sets of pillows for one person? Are you going to use 300 hand soaps ever fully? Will purchasing 2 bulk quantity of paper towels benefit you now or in the future?

# Chapter 8: Reframing Negative Thought Patterns

We all have negative core beliefs that haunt us each and every day. This worksheet below will show you how you can reframe those negative core belief systems to create a happier positive core belief.

By starting with one core belief that is negative and affects your life in a major way you can begin to declutter your mind of those negative thoughts that hold you back from completing goals and accomplishing things. On the next page is a worksheet that I have designed to help you work through all of these negative core beliefs that are harming you.

Negative frames of mind or stories that have affected you in the past can be harming your progress now. It is difficult to work through situations in life if all you see is the negative.

Many of our life stories are based on core beliefs that are negative and un-serving. They usually lead us to a period of self-doubt, self-defeating emotions, and thoughts, as well as actions. It is similar to walking around with a storm cloud over your head and only your head. It can be lonely, and you will feel like you are being singled out. During these times you will repeatedly epitomize this negative triad called cognitive triad.

- Views of yourself that are negative

- Views of the world that are negative

- Views of your future that are negative.

To properly be able to reframe these negatives to a positive you will want to examine the statements that you make about yourself, the world, and the future and then modify them to be more positive. By eliminating the negative side of a situation, you can begin to remember the positive sides of that same situation. It is a reframing technique that many Psychologists have been practicing for years. This practice can also help you identify and reframe those negative thoughts that you will face during challenging situations, then you will be able to avoid the process by which you only see negative aspects of the situation.

## Consider what your core values are and how you can prioritize them.

Prioritize them by the type need that you have for these values.

- What values do you hold as an essential value for your lifestyle?

- What values are representative of your way of life and how you wish to be seen?

- Which of these values is an essential part

of supporting the needs that are necessary for your inner self?

## Consider these three processes to find your core values:

1. **Experiences that made an impact in your life**

    - Think about moments that made an impact on your life.

    - What was the most important thing that was happening to you at that time?

    - What was taking place within your life right then?

    - Which of your values are you honoring at this exact moment?

2. **Suppressed Values**

- **Consider the suppressed values that you have as well.**

- Take this list in the opposite direction and consider the suppressed values that you have.

- What was taking place within your life at this time?

- What were your feelings about the experience?

- What value are you allowing to be suppressed?

3. **Code of Conduct**

- What is your most important code of conduct that you wish to instill?

- How are you going to show your self-expression in a creative way? A health and vitality level that is strong? A love for adventure and a sense of excitement about life? Do you wish to surround yourself with beauty? Taking quality time to learn all there is to know?

- Which of these values will affect you personally and diminish your honor?

## Give your personal values richer context.

Be creative with the context that you are placing your personal values into:

- **Use inspiring vocabulary words**. Your brain is quick to delete as well as ignore those mundane or commonplace words.

- **Search for words which will evoke or trigger an *emotional response*.** These words will have much more meaningful and memorable meaning to you.

- **Play on the strengths that you have** while you are crafting your values.

- **Make the statements of value-rich as well as meaningful** to you this will inspire you to do more.

**Let your core values sit and then come back to them with an open mind.**

After you completed your core values list, walk away and let it sit for a while then revisit them at a later date. Sit down and review the list that you have made:

- How is each of these items making you feel?

- Do you see a consistency in who you are in relation to these values?

- How personal are they to you?

- Are these values consistent with how you feel on a daily basis? Or do you feel like they represent someone else?

- Check the rankings by prioritizing them. Are they placed in the proper order? Are they listed with the most important ones first? Is the order consistent?

There is not one thing that is final with life, and there are no negatives to this activity.

## What are core beliefs?

Core beliefs are those messages that are formed within your mind about the experiences that you have had and how you feel about yourself. Your subconscious mind will form beliefs around the situations that take place in your life and due to those situations, the beliefs may be negative. These messages that are negative will then embed themselves into your mind and become what you consider the truth about any given situation. They become what makes you the person you are, your foundational beliefs and knowledge of awareness. When you have positive experiences within your life you will experience a core belief that is more positive. A negative or traumatic experience will give you negative core beliefs.

## Shifting Your Core Beliefs to A Positive Core Belief

It is not that hard to shift those core beliefs form a negative to a positive. In fact, it is something you can do with a few simple steps. By changing the mindset with positive affirmations, you can begin to change the core belief that is negative to a more positive belief system. For instance, "I am not good enough." Can be reframed to "I am enough." This is a simple step by step process that can be utilized by everyone.

By reframing the negative to the positive you are able to create a core belief that is much more supportive of a positive outlook and view. By having positive thoughts, you can start to make positive changes in your life.

## Core beliefs deeply affect you.

You will be deeply affected by your core beliefs. Once you have reframed your core beliefs you will be able to root them into your subconscious and be able to have significant changes in your life. The process of conveying positive self-images will help you govern your confidence, feelings, skillfulness, and the feelings of fulfillment and completeness.

## Negative core beliefs will deeply affect your life.

However, negative core beliefs can be the basis for a life of defeat and minimizing yourself. You will face doubt in yourself and your abilities to thrive in the world. You will also be more judgmental of yourself and you will tend to beat yourself up often about the fails within your life. This can result in a life-long habit of self-sabotage and disappointment. This can prevent you from success, fulfillment in life, and even achieving personal goals that you have set. They can alienate you from friends and family as well as make your lonely, undeserving, and stupid. Old beliefs that are negative can affect your entire life and you may not even know it.

## 3 Ways to Change These Core Beliefs

Simply change your negative beliefs to positive beliefs and this will help to change the outcome of your life. You may think that this is hard, and honestly it is quite hard to change how we think about ourselves. But with a little bit of practice and constant dedication to changing our core beliefs then you can begin to find a more positive spin on how you feel about your life and yourself. Below I have walked you through these simple steps that must be taken to begin this positive mindset shift.

## If you do not know what to fix, then you cannot fix it.

You must discover what is affecting you and then begin to fix it. Using a journal and write down all the core beliefs that you wish to change on the left-hand side of the paper. Make sure you list all of the core beliefs no matter how big or how small they are. They can be negative or positive it does not matter.

## Examine the list and decide if the ones you are looking at are your truth.

Your core beliefs can stop you from being able to love yourself and can make you extremely vulnerable to those that would take advantage of you. This will lead to self-judgment, self-destructive type behaviors, and negative self-talk. Mark the ones that are not your truth. This would be core beliefs that are false or even harmful—the ones that you would need to set a barrier with and walk away from so that you can achieve what you want in life. This will be the ones that you will need to focus on for the time being. These should be changed to reflect your truths.

## Shift your core beliefs into ones that are no longer harmful.

Shifting your core beliefs into ones that do not harm you anymore is key to changing your mindset. You must reframe them so that they are more positive and less destructive to your life. Write all of the core beliefs that are being reframed into a more positive core belief. This should be placed on the right-hand side of the core belief that was not positive.

## List the positive core beliefs on another piece of paper.

In order to embed your core beliefs into your

subconscious, you will have to practice, practice, practice. This will help you start a new daily habit of repeating the core beliefs that are lifting you up. Repeat this list every day, first thing in the morning and last thing at night. Then repeat them at least 8more times throughout the day. Continue to repeat this list for a total of 60 days. After 60 days your new belief system will be re-scripted from the negative beliefs. You do not have to fully believe it you simply need to repeat these over and over again so that you eventually will believe it.

## Working Towards Goals That Will Improve Your Life

Once you start to work towards these goals, you will be able to improve your life and make better decisions. By working on your goals, you can reach a level of growth that will help you achieve more things in your life.

Once you have identified the positive core beliefs that you wish to hold on to it is important to start using positive thinking techniques to instill them into your mindset on a more permanent basis. The more you repeat these positive thoughts and affirmations to yourself the more you will begin to change your core beliefs to a positive mindset.

## Strategies to Practice Positive Thinking

Positive thinking starts with a beginner's mindset. It is super easy to assume that you will not be able to accomplish something but to go into a project with a positive mindset means that you will have to work hard at maintaining the mindset.

Take deep breaths as you work through this process and maintain a calm mind. Empty everything from your mind and try to be as conscious as you can about the goals that you are setting. Believe that everything will work out for the best.

Create a list of the personal values that you have and maintain those values through everything that you do. This should be something that you sit down and figure out on your own. A pre-determined list of values may not be the same things that you value in your life. So, take some time with this and be specific.

# Chapter 9: Creating Healthier Routines and Daily Habits for Anxiety and Stress Relief

## Scheduling a New Daily Routine

By scheduling a daily routine, you can begin to make changes in your life that will help with decluttering your mind and space. A daily routine is built on all the things that you need to complete throughout the day such as:

- Waking up
- Showering
- Watching the news
- Eating breakfast
- Checking social media
- Checking email
- Reading a book
- Preparing your lunch

- Driving to work
- Working
- Taking lunch
- Driving home
- Preparing dinner
- Eating dinner
- And anything else that you do regularly throughout your day.

With a new daily schedule, you can eliminate the things in your life that are creating clutter and chaos and begin to incorporate new daily activities into your day that will better serve you in the long run. It is a simple process that many people are using to fit new activities into their already-busy schedules—the only difference with you is that you will be scheduling your pre-existing activities into your life with a less cluttered and chaotic or overwhelming effect.

To start off with, you will need to chart your daily activities' schedule. You can use the chart within the back of this book or another one of your choosing. It doesn't matter which chart you use as long as it makes sense to you.

## Daily Activities

Chart your day as a two-hour span of time. I have started my chart at 6 am. This can be started at any time that you are already waking up. For each two-hour span you will need to fill in the 5-minute increments under the start time and then proceed to fill in what you did each day of that week, minus this charting process. - since this is to just show how much time you spend wasting or in inactive stress reduction activities.

Now that you have your chart, you are going to begin to fill in every single 5-minute increment with what you are doing at that time. If the activity that you are doing takes up a bigger section of time, then five minutes then you will just fill it in to and draw a line to the amount of time it took you. This will show that space occupied by an activity. Once you have a weeks' worth of charting you should be able to sit back and look at all the activities that you are taking part in that are inactive ways to de-stress. From the previous chapter on stress, you know that these activities that are inactive are actually creating more stress and clutter within your life. So, your next goal is to create a routine that will take you out of the inactive and into the active.

This does not mean that you need to eliminate all of the inactive ways that you do de-stressing. We all love to watch TV. However, you will need to cut back on those times that are only creating more of the problem. This can be done by limiting those times. This will help you to begin a much healthier and more beneficial daily routine that will create lasting changes in your clutter and stress levels.

**Managing Daily Tasks**

This is an easy thing to do once you know exactly

what it is that you need to manage. Many people fill their days with activities that do not push them forward or simply clutter up their minds. This can be seen in the amount of sleep you are not getting. The amount of clutter you have in your home can show how cluttered you are inside. You can also show your stress levels by the amount of work that you are not getting done. When we stress out or live in a cluttered mindset you will feel as if you are accomplishing things in your day, but you will also feel like there is still so much to do.

You may be getting small tasks done but you are not fully immersing yourself in those tasks and completing then the way that they should be done. For instance, you may prepare dinner, but you may have forgotten about the laundry that was sitting in the washer. This creates another task to do when you realize that you have no work clothes washed and the ones that are in the wash are actually now mildewing. Another example of this would be reading a book for a class that you have to take for work. You are sitting there reading the book, but because your mind is in 100 places, you are not fully immersed in the book—and you have now forgotten the last pages' content and will need to reread that whole page. This is a clear example of a cluttered mind.

If you find yourself laying down at night to go to bed and going through a mental checklist of every single thing that you were supposed to get done that day only to realize that some major activity was not completed on time. Then you are living with too much mental clutter and will benefit from a new daily schedule that is managed more efficiently.

To manage your daily schedule properly is not something that should make you more stressed out. It should simply just compliment your already existing commitments. The difference in the cluttered chaotic schedule that you currently living, and a healthy managed schedule that you will be developing, is that your managed schedule will be much easier to work with and you will feel less clutter and chaos throughout your day. You will be able to sleep better, and you will find the confidence to complete more tasks in a timely manner.

By managing your schedule, you can begin to decrease those times within your schedule when you are being inactive and fill them in with active times. For instance, first thing in the morning you decide to spend 30 minutes working on your self-care. This can be done by waking at 6 am and then completing a series of activities that are building you up instead of tearing you down.

Hence, following this idea lets place a 30-minute self-care routine into the morning daily schedule. You will want to do the same activities every day so that it becomes a new habit. This will help with that overwhelm and clutter that you feel early in the morning when you have woken up late and know that your day will be not so great because you did not start your day on time. Those moments when you feel like everything is just overwhelming, and there is too much clutter inside.

By incorporating this simple change into your morning routine, you can begin to make changes in your life that will help you reduce the clutter and stress that you are feeling inside. Once you have developed a schedule that works for you in the morning, you will want to carry that over throughout your day. Incorporating positive changes into your day. One way to do this is to fill in all the times that you would otherwise be overwhelmed or chaotic with more calming activities.

For instance, those moments when you come in the form a long day at work and you are stressed out or tired, consider tossing a load of laundry in the washing machine and then doing a 30-minute yoga session, instead of plopping down on the couch to watch mindless TV. After you have completed a 30-minute session of yoga you will have more energy to work on other activities that are needed to be done on that day.

Try to incorporate less TV and social media time into your day and spend more time in activities that will declutter and de-stress you. If you have a long list of to-dos on a daily basis that you never seem to get to the bottom of, then consider writing down all the things that you have to do, and starting with the easiest ones, make a 3 task a day list until you have reduced your list by half. Every day you should work on 3 tasks. Starting with the easiest ones will give you the momentum and confidence to accomplish the big ones when it comes time to. This is a process that helps you eliminate tasks in a timely manner without overwhelming your day.

## Developing a New Routine With a Handy Workbook

The best way to develop a new routine is to use the handy chart and workbook that I have provided at the end of this book. Each simple step that I have gone over will bring you a step closer to decluttering your mind and reaching a less chaotic, less stressful lifestyle.

The first thing I talked about was decreasing your sense of overwhelm from social media. I went over how you can chart your social media habits and then use those to charts to develop a plan that would be more beneficial and less overwhelming. Then I talked about ways that you can reduce the stress by incorporating more active stress reduction activities into your day, such as meditation, journaling, gratitude, exercise, self-care routines, engaging the mind by reading, and creating a better morning routine.

The next part of decluttering your mind that I talked about is decluttering those toxic relationships. Eliminating those in your life that are creating negative barriers to your success. Finally, I discussed how to declutter those negative thoughts that come into your mind and how to reframe them to be more positive and uplifting. Then I discussed how you can manage your daily routine with ease and using a chart to map out your daily activities.

At the end of this chapter, I will include all the workbook sections for you to print off and begin to utilize for your daily activities and decluttering your mind and life.

# Be more active and stress less, gain more sleep, and live with less clutter

Being active is a great way to increase your heart rate, decrease your stress levels and be a much healthier person. There are so many ways that you can get healthy and active and below is a listing of several of them. By adding exercise to your day, you are able to maintain a practice of building muscle mass, as well as increasing the blood flow and lowering your stress levels. This helps to keep you calmer and more alert throughout the day. With today's lifestyles being so sedentary it is a great idea to incorporate exercise into your daily routine. Spend time outside with your family and friends or your pet. Get fresh air and expand your adventures and horizons with some well-needed exercise. Go for a hike in the mountains or simply take a walk in the park. These are all great options for adding exercise to your day. Exercising has a way of decreasing depression and raising your confidence.

**Go for walks.**

Walks are a great way to get tons of exercise. They also allow you to decompress. They boost your motivation. Find a way to incorporate more walks into your day. Find a friend to walk with you during the day. Take a walk to the local park for the kids to play.

**Take the stairs.**

Choose to take the stairs instead of the elevator. This will increase your endorphins and also reduce your stress. The stairs will add an extra cardio workout to your already existing exercise routine. It will also tone and maximize your butt muscles.

## Clean vigorously.

Clean your house more vigorously on those days that you cannot get out to get more exercise. When you make useful time with your cleaning schedule you can take a more aggressive role in your cleaning and get some really great exercise in.

## Use a basket instead of a shopping cart.

If you only have a minor number of things to collect at the grocery store, then using a smaller cart or basket will help you gain some exercise. This makes it an automatic session of lifting weights since you will be carrying the heavy basket. The more stuff you put into the basket the heavier it will get, and this will provide a free weight to lift so that you can gain muscle mass in your arms. It also creates a resistance exercise.

## Park further away from the entrance to the store.

Park further from the door so that you have longer to walk and gain some cardio. This will not only help you burn calories but also protect your car more since it is parked where most people will not park. By parking further out in the parking lot you will start to spend more time walking to your car and into the store than you would if you parked at the door. This creates a simple exercise that can help you gain more healthy exercise.

## Play outside with your pets.

Pets are a great way to get more exercise in your day. Take them for a walk, play with them in the park. Chase them in your yard. If you have a local dog park, consider heading to the dog park everyday on a set time period so that your dog will start to hold you accountable. For instance, if you are taking your dog for a walk everyday at 9 am then your dog's biological clock will recognize that time and come to you at the exact time to go for a walk. This helps you have a sort of notification for the dogs walking time, and also allows you to take the time off of work that is needed for that necessary break.

## Clean while you are talking on the phone.

Phone calls can make you complacent so instead of sitting down, clean your house. This is a bit of multitasking, however—this form of multitasking does not require full brain power for both activities. Many times, you will find yourself on the phone and you will begin to hang your laundry or clean your kitchen. This is a way of occupying your mind and your body at the same time. It is a great way to get exercise and communicate with friends and family.

## Exercise often while you are watching TV.

When there are moments that you are watching

television, you should spend that time running or doing some form of exercise. This will help you kill two birds with one stone. If you have access to a treadmill or a stationary bike you can use this while watching TV so that you are getting exercise while also watching your favorite TV shows. It may even be a good idea to move your TV into the exercise room so that every time you go to watch TV your drawn to exercise.

## Support a good cause and do a walk or run.

There is always some charity going on that would give your exercise. You can volunteer as a coordinator or you can participate in the walk or run. By supporting something that you feel strongly about you are not only getting exercise, but you are also feeding that need that everyone has for helping others and being involved with a community of like-minded individuals. Support a worthy cause and feel better about your life and the lives of those around you.

## Supplements provide a great way to maximize your health and create a protective barrier for stress.

Supplements are a great way to improve your health and eliminate the effects of stress on the body. There are several supplements that can help with anxiety reduction. Below is a brief summary of them.

**Kava Kava**: psychoactive member, pepper family, sedative, mild stress and anxiety relief

**Lemon balm**: mint family, anti-anxiety effects

Omega-3 Fatty acids: studies show a 20% reduction in the anxiety of patients.

**Valerian**: sleep aid, tranquilizing effect, valerenic acid, alter gamma-aminobutyric acid, lowers anxiety

**Green tea**: contains polyphenol antioxidants, lowers stress and anxiety, with increased serotonin

**Ashwagandha:** Ayurvedic medicine, stress and anxiety, studies show the effectiveness of it.

With all the available options in the world today for supplements, exercise routines, and healthy food it is surprising that more people are not de-stressing and creating a healthier lifestyle. By decluttering your life of all the unnecessary inactive activities that are creating more stress and anxiety in your life you are able to live a fuller happier life.

# Conclusion

Now that you have completed this book, you can begin to download all of the pages for the workbook and start to work towards a decluttered life. This book has been filled with details to help you understand what a cluttered mind is and how you can begin to declutter your mind. As an adult, I imagine that you get so busy trying to do all kinds of things for other people that you sometimes forget to do the most important things that you need. Through this overwhelm of activity you will find that you are not Superwoman or Superman. You cannot do all the things that others expect from you if you do not take care of yourself first. for People will constantly come into your life and expect you to handle their responsibilities and by learning to say no to them and yes to you, you can begin to declutter, de-stress, and reorganize your life in some healthy ways.

When you try to complete all kinds of tasks and goals, while worrying about everyone else's duties and responsibilities, you will begin to cause yourself more harm than good. Often times, people will think that the more they get done in the day the less they will have to follow up with in the future. They will busy themselves with overwhelming amounts of activity and clutter in their mind and eventually burn out from the constant distractions from their own personal needs. It can become a hard lesson to learn but often it is one that everyone must learn in order to start taking proper care of their life, mind, body, and soul.

To be healthy you must live healthy. That includes saying no to others who are delegating their responsibilities to you, getting healthy habits established within your life, being active in exercise and creating a less cluttered environment, and taking care to be more positive in your thoughts, mindset, feelings, and actions towards others. By saying no to other people's responsibilities, you are being a much better friend than if you would simply take on the task and then resent them later for asking you.

If you have made it to this point of the book, then you know that clutter in your mind can harm you in so many medical ways. Not only can it create large amounts of stress, but it can cause you to have mental health issues as well. Cluttering up your thoughts and mind has been a leading cause of stress related anxieties, health problems that affect the heart, body, and mind, as well as the damage that is done to relationships. When effectively decluttering your mind and your lifestyle you have to learn what is not creating positive actions in your life and then find ways to reframe them of release them into the world. To be free from clutter means so much more than you can imagine and once you start to move beyond the clutter you will begin to see positive changes in not only yourself, but the environment that you live in and the people that you share your life with.

Clutter is the leading culprit to stress-related health concerns. By keeping tabs on your stress, you can reduce the amount that you have to deal with over time. There are so many things in our lives that are contributing to our stress. When we spend too much time trying to complete tasks that we will not accomplish, we are causing ourselves more stress. When you do not eat right, you are causing yourself more stress. When you are overwhelmed by social media or social interactions, you are causing yourself more stress. There are so many things that can cause you stress—and due to clutter in your mind, you can get stuck in a rut of continued stress and aggravation.

Although this book is about clutter in your mind, the clutter in your home is just as bad. If you are living in an environment that is full of junk, then you can believe that your mind is just as cluttered. Over time, you will begin to develop even more complications in life due to the clutter that you have built up in your mind and your home. By having a cluttered home environment, you will begin to develop sever bouts of anxiety, depression, isolation, stress, fear of loss and change and so much more. Clutter has been known to create mental health problems or intensify already existing ones.

Below, I have included a work book that is downloadable, which I designed for you to use. These worksheets are easy to use and can help you work through the clutter that has been piling up in your mind and your life. Each page within this section of worksheets is specifically designed for a special reason. By reading the book you will be able to complete these worksheets and effectively begin to change your life for the better. Once you have completed reading the book, then you can download the workbook and start making your life better.

Keep this book handy any time you begin to face overwhelm, stress, clutter or changes in your life that need to be addressed in this same manner as laid out in the book. Also keep this book handy for when you declutter your life. Each step can be found within these pages and by carefully studying the pages in this book you will be able to create growth and change in your life.

Everyone deserves to change the things in their life that creates stress. They deserve to have less clutter and more focus. They deserve to be healthier, less disorganized, more active, and much more goal oriented. By determining the actions in your life that are creating the clutter that you are struggling with you will be able to make those changes that will impact your life for the future and also teach you how to continue this growth and change for a lifetime.

# Workbook

## Social Media Chart

| Times | Monday | Tuesday | Wednesday | Thursday | Friday | Saturday | Sunday |
|---|---|---|---|---|---|---|---|
| 6 am | | | | | | | |
| 8 am | | | | | | | |
| 10 am | | | | | | | |
| 12 pm | | | | | | | |
| 2 pm | | | | | | | |
| 4 pm | | | | | | | |
| 6 pm | | | | | | | |
| 8 pm | | | | | | | |
| 10 pm | | | | | | | |

# **Social Media Chart (example)**

| Times | Monday | Tuesday | Wednesday | Thursday | Friday | Saturday | Sunday |
|---|---|---|---|---|---|---|---|
| 6 am | Instagram 20 Facebook 30 Pinterest 10 Twitter 5 | | Instagram 20 Facebook 30 Pinterest 10 Twitter 5 | | Instagram 20 Facebook 30 Pinterest 10 Twitter 5 | | Instagram 20 Facebook 30 Pinterest 10 Twitter 5 |
| 8 am | | Instagram 20 Facebook 30 Pinterest 10 Twitter 5 | | Instagram 20 Facebook 30 Pinterest 10 Twitter 5 | Instagram 10 Facebook 30 Pinterest 30 Twitter 25 | | Instagram 50 Facebook 20 Pinterest 0 Twitter 25 |
| 10 am | Instagram 30 Facebook 15 Pinterest 30 Twitter 15 | | Instagram 55 Facebook 30 Pinterest 10 Twitter 5 | | | Instagram 20 Facebook 40 Pinterest 10 Twitter 5 | |
| 12 pm | Instagram 1hr 20 Facebook Pinterest 30 Twitter 5 | Instagram 10 Facebook 30 Pinterest 30 Twitter 5 | | | Instagram 40 Facebook 1hr 30 Pinterest 10 Twitter 15 | | |

| | | | | | | | |
|---|---|---|---|---|---|---|---|
| 2 pm | | Instagram 1hr Facebook 40 Pinterest 10 Twitter 25 | Instagram 60 Facebook 40 Pinterest 0 Twitter 25 | Instagram 10 Facebook 30 Pinterest 10 Twitter 5 | | Instagram 20 Facebook 30 Pinterest 10 Twitter 5 | Instagram 20 Facebook ok Pinterest 1hr Twitter 5 |
| 4 pm | | | | Instagram 45 Facebook 20 Pinterest 10 Twitter 5 | | Instagram Facebook Pinterest 2hr Twitter | |
| 6 pm | Instagram Facebook 1hr 40 Pinterest 10 Twitter 5 | | | | Instagram 1hr 5min Facebook Pinterest Twitter | | Instagram Facebook 1hr 40 Pinterest 10 Twitter 20 |
| 8 pm | | | Instagram 2 hr. Facebook Pinterest Twitter | | | | |
| 10 pm | | Instagram Facebook 2hr Pinterest Twitter | | | Instagram 2hr Facebook Pinterest Twitter | Instagram 2hr Facebook Pinterest Twitter | |

# Negative Core Beliefs Worksheet

| Negative Core Beliefs | |
|---|---|
| Negative Belief that you wish to adjust: | |
| The percentage of how much you believe this negative belief: (0-100%) | |
| How do you feel about this at this time: | |
| At what time is this negative belief most believable: | |
| At what time is the negative belief less believable: | |
| What are the emotions that are connected to this belief: | |
| A new core belief that is balanced and positive that you wish to apply and adopt: | |
| How much do you believe this to be true at this moment: (0-100%) | |
| How are you feeling about this at this time? | |

| At what time is this positive balanced belief most convincing: | |
|---|---|
| At what time is this positive balanced belief least convincing: | |
| What are the emotions that come up with this belief: | |

# Negative Core Beliefs Worksheet (example 1)

| Negative Core Beliefs | |
|---|---|
| Negative Belief that you wish to adjust: | I am not enough |
| The percentage of how much you believe this negative belief: (0-100%) | 46% |
| How do you feel about this at this time: | Saddened by this belief |
| At what time is this negative belief most believable: | When I am feeling down about myself |
| At what time is the negative belief less believable: | When spending time with others and accomplishing goals |
| What are the emotions that are connected to this belief: | I feel saddened by it |
| A new core belief that is balanced and positive that you wish to apply and adopt: | I am enough |
| How much do you believe this to be true at this moment: (0-100%) | 56% |

| | |
|---|---|
| How are you feeling about this at this time? | Happier and more encouraged |
| At what time is this positive balanced belief most convincing: | When I am knocking things out of the park |
| At what time is this positive balanced belief least convincing: | When things are not going well and I am failing at my goals. |
| What are the emotions that come up with this belief: | Happier and more accomplished |

# Negative Core Beliefs Worksheet (example 2)

| Negative Core Beliefs | |
|---|---|
| Negative Belief that you wish to adjust: | That I am not deserving of money |
| The percentage of how much you believe this negative belief: (0-100%) | 54% |
| How do you feel about this at this time: | Beaten and worthless |
| At what time is this negative belief most believable: | When it is hard to make ends meet |
| At what time is the negative belief less believable: | When I am crushing it with work |
| What are the emotions that are connected to this belief: | Like a failure who is broke |
| A new core belief that is balanced and positive that you wish to apply and adopt: | That I deserve to make money and have clients |
| How much do you believe this to be true at this moment: (0-100%) | 54% |

| How are you feeling about this at this time? | Happier and more accomplished |
|---|---|
| At what time is this positive balanced belief most convincing: | When I am crushing it with my business |
| At what time is this positive balanced belief least convincing: | When I am failing at work |
| What are the emotions that come up with this belief: | That I am worthwhile |

# Managing Daily Tasks

| Times | Monday | Tuesday | Wednesday | Thursday | Friday | Saturday | Sunday |
|---|---|---|---|---|---|---|---|
| 6 am | | | | | | | |
| 6:05 | | | | | | | |
| 6:10 | | | | | | | |
| 6:15 | | | | | | | |
| 6:20 | | | | | | | |
| 6:25 | | | | | | | |
| 6:30 | | | | | | | |
| 6:35 | | | | | | | |
| 6:40 | | | | | | | |
| 6:45 | | | | | | | |
| 6:50 | | | | | | | |
| 6:55 | | | | | | | |
| 7 am | | | | | | | |
| 7:05 | | | | | | | |
| 7:10 | | | | | | | |
| 7:15 | | | | | | | |
| 7:20 | | | | | | | |
| 7:25 | | | | | | | |
| 7:30 | | | | | | | |
| 7:35 | | | | | | | |
| 7:40 | | | | | | | |
| 7:45 | | | | | | | |
| 7:50 | | | | | | | |
| 7:55 | | | | | | | |

| Time | | | | | | | |
|---|---|---|---|---|---|---|---|
| 8 am | | | | | | | |
| 8:05 | | | | | | | |
| 8:10 | | | | | | | |
| 8:15 | | | | | | | |
| 8:20 | | | | | | | |
| 8:25 | | | | | | | |
| 8:30 | | | | | | | |
| 8:35 | | | | | | | |
| 8:40 | | | | | | | |
| 8:45 | | | | | | | |
| 8:50 | | | | | | | |
| 8:55 | | | | | | | |
| 9am | | | | | | | |
| 9:05 | | | | | | | |
| 9:10 | | | | | | | |
| 9:15 | | | | | | | |
| 9:20 | | | | | | | |
| 9:25 | | | | | | | |
| 9:30 | | | | | | | |
| 9:35 | | | | | | | |
| 9:40 | | | | | | | |
| 9:45 | | | | | | | |
| 9:50 | | | | | | | |
| 9:55 | | | | | | | |

| | | | | | | | |
|---|---|---|---|---|---|---|---|
| 10 am | | | | | | | |
| 10:05 | | | | | | | |
| 10:10 | | | | | | | |
| 10:15 | | | | | | | |
| 10:20 | | | | | | | |
| 10:25 | | | | | | | |
| 10:30 | | | | | | | |
| 10:35 | | | | | | | |
| 10:40 | | | | | | | |
| 10:45 | | | | | | | |
| 10:50 | | | | | | | |
| 10:55 | | | | | | | |
| 11 am | | | | | | | |
| 11:05 | | | | | | | |
| 11:10 | | | | | | | |
| 11:15 | | | | | | | |
| 11:20 | | | | | | | |
| 11:25 | | | | | | | |
| 11:30 | | | | | | | |
| 11:35 | | | | | | | |
| 11:40 | | | | | | | |
| 11:45 | | | | | | | |
| 11:50 | | | | | | | |
| 11:55 | | | | | | | |

| | | | | | | | |
|---|---|---|---|---|---|---|---|
| 12 pm | | | | | | | |
| 12:05 | | | | | | | |
| 12:10 | | | | | | | |
| 12:15 | | | | | | | |
| 12:20 | | | | | | | |
| 12:25 | | | | | | | |
| 12:30 | | | | | | | |
| 12:35 | | | | | | | |
| 12:40 | | | | | | | |
| 12:45 | | | | | | | |
| 12:50 | | | | | | | |
| 12:55 | | | | | | | |
| 1 pm | | | | | | | |
| 1:05 | | | | | | | |
| 1:10 | | | | | | | |
| 1:15 | | | | | | | |
| 1:20 | | | | | | | |
| 1:25 | | | | | | | |
| 1:30 | | | | | | | |
| 1:35 | | | | | | | |
| 1:40 | | | | | | | |
| 1:45 | | | | | | | |
| 1:50 | | | | | | | |
| 1:55 | | | | | | | |

| | | | | | | | |
|---|---|---|---|---|---|---|---|
| 2 pm | | | | | | | |
| 2:05 | | | | | | | |
| 2:10 | | | | | | | |
| 2:15 | | | | | | | |
| 2:20 | | | | | | | |
| 2:25 | | | | | | | |
| 2:30 | | | | | | | |
| 2:35 | | | | | | | |
| 2:40 | | | | | | | |
| 2:45 | | | | | | | |
| 2:50 | | | | | | | |
| 2:55 | | | | | | | |
| 3 pm | | | | | | | |
| 3:05 | | | | | | | |
| 3:10 | | | | | | | |
| 3:15 | | | | | | | |
| 3:20 | | | | | | | |
| 3:25 | | | | | | | |
| 3:30 | | | | | | | |
| 3:35 | | | | | | | |
| 3:40 | | | | | | | |
| 3:45 | | | | | | | |
| 3:50 | | | | | | | |
| 3:55 | | | | | | | |

| | | | | | | | | |
|---|---|---|---|---|---|---|---|---|
| 4 pm | | | | | | | | |
| 4:05 | | | | | | | | |
| 4:10 | | | | | | | | |
| 4:15 | | | | | | | | |
| 4:20 | | | | | | | | |
| 4:25 | | | | | | | | |
| 4:30 | | | | | | | | |
| 4:35 | | | | | | | | |
| 4:40 | | | | | | | | |
| 4:45 | | | | | | | | |
| 4:50 | | | | | | | | |
| 4:55 | | | | | | | | |
| 5 pm | | | | | | | | |
| 5:05 | | | | | | | | |
| 5:10 | | | | | | | | |
| 5:15 | | | | | | | | |
| 5:20 | | | | | | | | |
| 5:25 | | | | | | | | |
| 5:30 | | | | | | | | |
| 5:35 | | | | | | | | |
| 5:40 | | | | | | | | |
| 5:45 | | | | | | | | |
| 5:50 | | | | | | | | |
| 5:55 | | | | | | | | |

| | | | | | | | | |
|---|---|---|---|---|---|---|---|---|
| 6 pm | | | | | | | | |
| 6:05 | | | | | | | | |
| 6:10 | | | | | | | | |
| 6:15 | | | | | | | | |
| 6:20 | | | | | | | | |
| 6:25 | | | | | | | | |
| 6:30 | | | | | | | | |
| 6:35 | | | | | | | | |
| 6:40 | | | | | | | | |
| 6:45 | | | | | | | | |
| 6:50 | | | | | | | | |
| 6:55 | | | | | | | | |
| 7 pm | | | | | | | | |
| 7:05 | | | | | | | | |
| 7:10 | | | | | | | | |
| 7:15 | | | | | | | | |
| 7:20 | | | | | | | | |
| 7:25 | | | | | | | | |
| 7:30 | | | | | | | | |
| 7:35 | | | | | | | | |
| 7:40 | | | | | | | | |
| 7:45 | | | | | | | | |
| 7:50 | | | | | | | | |
| 7:55 | | | | | | | | |

| | | | | | | | |
|---|---|---|---|---|---|---|---|
| 8 pm | | | | | | | |
| 8:05 | | | | | | | |
| 8:10 | | | | | | | |
| 8:15 | | | | | | | |
| 8:20 | | | | | | | |
| 8:25 | | | | | | | |
| 8:30 | | | | | | | |
| 8:35 | | | | | | | |
| 8:40 | | | | | | | |
| 8:45 | | | | | | | |
| 8:50 | | | | | | | |
| 8:55 | | | | | | | |
| 9pm | | | | | | | |
| 9:05 | | | | | | | |
| 9:10 | | | | | | | |
| 9:15 | | | | | | | |
| 9:20 | | | | | | | |
| 9:25 | | | | | | | |
| 9:30 | | | | | | | |
| 9:35 | | | | | | | |
| 9:40 | | | | | | | |
| 9:45 | | | | | | | |
| 9:50 | | | | | | | |
| 9:55 | | | | | | | |

| | | | | | | | |
|---|---|---|---|---|---|---|---|
| 10 pm | | | | | | | |
| 10:05 | | | | | | | |
| 10:10 | | | | | | | |
| 10:15 | | | | | | | |
| 10:20 | | | | | | | |
| 10:25 | | | | | | | |
| 10:30 | | | | | | | |
| 10:35 | | | | | | | |
| 10:40 | | | | | | | |
| 10:45 | | | | | | | |
| 10:50 | | | | | | | |
| 10:55 | | | | | | | |
| 11 pm | | | | | | | |
| 11:05 | | | | | | | |
| 11:10 | | | | | | | |
| 11:15 | | | | | | | |
| 11:20 | | | | | | | |
| 11:25 | | | | | | | |
| 11:30 | | | | | | | |
| 11:35 | | | | | | | |
| 11:40 | | | | | | | |
| 11:45 | | | | | | | |
| 11:50 | | | | | | | |
| 11:55 | | | | | | | |

## Managing Daily Tasks (example)

| Times | Monday | Tuesday | Wednesday | Thursday | Friday | Saturday | Sunday |
|---|---|---|---|---|---|---|---|
| 6 am | Wake | Wake | Wake | Wake | Wake | Wake | Wake |
| 6:05 | Wash face and body Journal Gratitude Mediation Read 10 min. Check your daily schedule Proceed with your day | Wash face and body Journal Gratitude Mediation Read 10 min. Check your daily schedule Proceed with your day | Wash face and body Journal Gratitude Mediation Read 10 min. Check your daily schedule Proceed with your day | Wash face and body Journal Gratitude Mediation Read 10 min. Check your daily schedule Proceed with your day | Wash face and body Journal Gratitude Mediation Read 10 min. Check your daily schedule Proceed with your day | Wash face and body Journal Gratitude Mediation Read 10 min. Check your daily schedule Proceed with your day | Wash face and body Journal Gratitude Mediation Read 10 min. Check your daily schedule Proceed with your day |
| 6:10 | | | | | | | |
| 6:15 | | | | | | | |
| 6:20 | | | | | | | |
| 6:25 | | | | | | | |
| 6:30 | | | | | | | |
| 6:35 | | | | | | | |
| 6:40 | | | | | | | |
| 6:45 | | | | | | | |
| 6:50 | | | | | | | |
| 6:55 | | | | | | | |
| 7 am | | | | | | | |
| 7:05 | | | | | | | |
| 7:10 | | | | | | | |
| 7:15 | | | | | | | |
| 7:20 | | | | | | | |
| 7:25 | | | | | | | |
| 7:30 | | | | | | | |
| 7:35 | | | | | | | |
| 7:40 | | | | | | | |
| 7:45 | | | | | | | |
| 7:50 | | | | | | | |
| 7:55 | | | | | | | |

# Negative to Positive Thinking

| Negative Phrase or Core Belief | Reframing to Positive Affirmation |
|---|---|
| | |
| | |
| | |
| | |
| | |
| | |
| | |
| | |
| | |
| | |

## Negative to Positive Thinking (example)

| Negative Phrase or Core Belief | Reframing to Positive Affirmation |
|---|---|
| "I am not good enough." | "I am enough." |
| "I do not deserve anything." | "I deserve all the world has to offer." |
| "I'm so stupid." | "I am brilliant." |
| | |

# About the Author

Mary Connor is a professional organizer, a wife and mom to three children, a cleaning expert, and a former finance manager. She is passionate about helping people lead better lives and shares easy and inexpensive organizing tips and tricks on how to clean up life's little and big messes. In addition, she teaches women how to pay off debts, improve their money management skills and increase their wealth.

In the past, Mary found her passion in writing and focuses on topics that can make a real difference in helping others accomplish their goals and dreams. She has made it a habit to continue learning new things so that she can share these insights with the world in a concise and helpful way. This interest has led her to the life of learning several factors affecting human interactions. Moreover, she continually works on expanding her knowledge by attending seminars and networking with other professionals.

Mary loves the outdoors and likes to walk or run every day. She is dedicated to the practice of mindfulness and feels that a minimalist lifestyle is important to both success and happiness. When not writing or walking, Mary enjoys spending time horseback riding with her daughters or relaxing at the lake with her husband.

CPSIA information can be obtained
at www.ICGtesting.com
Printed in the USA
BVHW070726100219
539877BV00001B/151/P